Guy de Maupassant

Boule de Suif

Peggy Chaplin

Lecturer in French,
University of Keele

University of Glasgow French and German Publications
1988

University of Glasgow French and German Publications

Series Editors: Mark G. Ward (German)
Geoff Woollen (French)

Consultant Editors : Colin Smethurst
Kenneth Varty

Modern Languages Building, University of Glasgow,
Glasgow G12 8QL, Scotland.

First published 1988

Printed in Great Britain by BPCC Wheatons Ltd, Exeter

ISBN   0 85261 250 8

Contents

In memory of Paul Smith,
Lecturer in French,
Keele University,
1968-81

Foreword

Ever since its publication in 1880, *Boule de Suif* has received critical and popular acclaim. It has been praised as an exemplar of the art of short story writing, and continues to reward the researcher. The fact that it has appeared at the head of two different collections of Maupassant's works, one devoted to the Franco-Prussian war and the other to Normandy, underlines its twin foci of interest. Its enduring appeal to the reader is manifested by frequent republication and, for the English speaker, in retranslation.

This new study is aimed at the first-time reader of the French text looking for methods of approach. Students of French history and civilisation will find, in the introductory chapter on the Franco-Prussian war and the collapse of the Second Empire, information helpful to an understanding of the historical perspective, while the section on events surrounding the conduct of the war in Normandy brings the reader closer to Maupassant's original aim in writing the story.

Students of literary history will find a section on literary background dealing with Maupassant's fleeting acquaintance with Zola and the Naturalists, culminating in the publication of the *Soirées de Médan* , which is evaluated here. The other stories in the collection are discussed in the light of their relevance to themes in *Boule de Suif* .

Students of the text itself will find here, in the discussion of Structure, Narrative Techniques and Characterisation, analyses which reveal the dynamism of the work, together with a close critical commentary on its arresting beginning.

The page references to the text of *Boule de Suif* given here are to the Harrap edition by W.M. Landers, first published in 1982 as *Boule de Suif et autres contes de la guerre* .

Chapter One

The Franco-Prussian War of 1870-1871

THE SECOND EMPIRE (1852-1870)

Maupassant did not need, as is now necessary, to explain to his readers the background to the declaration of war between France and Prussia on 19 July 1870. Born in 1850, he had grown up with the Second Empire of Napoléon III, who had previously been president of the reconstituted Second Republic as Prince Louis-Napoléon until seizing power in a coup d'état in 1851. Declared emperor in 1852, Napoléon III, who was a nephew of Napoléon Bonaparte, represented the hopes of those who wished for a return to dynastic rule, but without the problems that had accompanied the restoration of the Bourbons (Louis XVIII and Charles X) or the Orleans branch of the family (Louis-Philippe). The emperor had therefore to reconcile the various strands of conservatism (Legitimists, Orleanists and Bonapartists) and at the same time retain the confidence of republican and radical tendencies in France.

Napoléon III endeavoured during his reign to achieve a balance of power in Europe which would work to France's benefit. His problem was to ensure that the German states, led by Prussia, did not totally dominate the ancient empire of Austria and thereby threaten French hopes for those parts of Italy under Austrian rule. At the same time, Austria must not become too powerful and drive the French out of Italy.

Thus Napoléon III's reign was characterised by a series of negotiations between European states, continually shifting ground in a cynical, if logical struggle for supremacy. It is hardly surprising if Napoléon III seemed to be, at least to some of his subjects, a dishonourable shuffler. Certainly his enemies seem to have understood his strategies of bluff and barter, and the Prussian chancellor, Count Otto von Bismarck, was finally able to ensure that

France had no allies in the Franco-Prussian war by revealing to other countries the secret claims laid to their territories by the Emperor.

The emperor and King Wilhelm of Prussia were no strangers to each other. Napoléon III had congratulated the King in person on his accession to the throne of Prussia, and in 1862 Count von Bismarck became Prussian ambassador to France, although he was recalled to Berlin after only a few months. In less than a decade, Bismarck's understanding of the emperor's tactics enabled him to ensure Prussian superiority and lay the foundations for German unity. Napoléon III himself had spent much of his early life in his mother's homes in Switzerland and Germany and spoke fluent German.

Nevertheless, in spite of personal connections, politics demanded that France and Prussia should execute complicated manoeuvres in their struggle for dominance. In 1863, hostilities broke out between Poland and Russia. The Prussians took the side of the Russians, so France had to support the Poles. In 1865, however, Prussia and Austria seemed to be close allies, and now France had to befriend Prussia in hopes of effecting a separation between that country and Austria. In 1866, the battle of Sadowa saw the Austrians convincingly beaten by the Prussians, and the French became mediators.

Napoléon III still cherished hopes of taming the Prussians and gaining German territory in the Rhineland. Heedless of the Prussian display of strength at Sadowa, his diplomatic moves show all too clearly the disastrous failure to recognise the aim of Bismarck's policies.

Not only was France politically unstable in its foreign policies, but at home too there was dissatisfaction. In 1864, the liberal minister Adolphe Thiers had succeeded in forcing the Emperor to grant certain freedoms to the press and parliament, as well as to the individual, and in 1869 the opposition won an election victory, thus obliging the emperor to accept the elaboration of a liberal constitution. In spite of this constitutional setback, a plebiscite held before the war, in 1870, produced a decisive vote in favour of the emperor.

The circumstances in which war was declared suggest that Napoléon III was not unfavourable to the idea of confrontation between France and Prussia, believing that Prussia would back down on such an occasion. The opportunity to assert French superiority arose when the throne of Spain fell vacant and a candidate from the Prussian royal family was proposed. The possibility of a Prussian stronghold beyond the Pyrenees caused an uproar in France. A diplomatic offensive was launched by sending Count Benedetti, the French ambassador, to obtain from King Wilhelm a declaration that he would never permit one of his family to accede to the throne of Spain. King Wilhelm was prepared to concede that the "Hohenzollern candidacy" should not go forward, and expressed this to the ambassador. The news arrived in Paris, where it was joyfully received. At this stage confrontation might have been avoided, but the Emperor Napoléon and his advisers decided that Prussia must admit publicly its withdrawal from the candidacy. Moreover, King Wilhelm should promise that no attempt would be made to renew the claim to the Spanish throne. Count Benedetti was sent back to Bad Ems to approach King Wilhelm on the 13 July. By now the king was irritated by the persistence of Benedetti, and apprehensive about the attitude of Chancellor Bismarck, who was threatening resignation over the affair. The king, refusing to act directly, sent a telegram to Bismarck in Berlin, with the request that he should communicate to France the Prussian rejection of France's continued interference.

It was the chance that Bismarck and the Prussian military had been waiting for. A carefully abbreviated version of the King's telegram was sent out to all Prussian embassies, and made public via the press. The intention was to humiliate and insult France, for the telegram now conveyed the message that the King of Prussia had snubbed the French ambassador, with the intention of breaking off relations between their two countries. The reaction from France that Bismarck and his colleagues had desired came quickly. In vain did Thiers protest that France was in grave danger, and French observers in Prussia issue warnings about the Prussian military machine prepared for war with France. The Emperor and his advisers responded to the challenge implicit in the telegram, and set out to defend the injured honour of France. War was declared on 19 July 1870.

The Prussians were joined by the southern states of Germany, so that it was indeed a German, not simply a Prussian force that invaded France in the shape of three armies, and proceeded to push back the poorly prepared and

3

provisioned line of French defence. By mid-August, the two French armies under MacMahon and Bazaine were split. Bazaine was trapped under siege in the city of Metz, and MacMahon's army, in trying to come to the aid of Bazaine, was intercepted at Sedan on 1 September.

Among the defeated there was the Emperor himself. He became the prisoner of the Prussians and accepted a period of detention (of the most regal kind) in Germany, before leaving for final exile in England. In the circumstances he had no choice but to abdicate, leaving the way clear for his ministers to form a "government of national defence" and to declare, on 4 September 1870, the founding of the Third Republic.

Under the presidency of General Trochu, the government voted to continue the war. On 15 September the siege of Paris began, and on 27 October Bazaine surrendered Metz, thus freeing Prussian forces to join in the attack on Paris. A new, "Army of the Loire" was rapidly formed, and fought valiantly; so too did the re-formed Army of the North, under General Faidherbe, but the isolation of Paris, after the German forces had overrun most of Northern France, obliged the French to surrender on 28 January 1871. France had lost some 150,000 men in the war. The frontier provinces of Alsace and Lorraine were to be handed over to the victors and heavy indemnities were to be paid.

When the peace conditions had been negotiated and signed, the German troops withdrew from Paris. Their departure acted as the signal to the supporters of radical left-wing politics to attempt to seize power in the capital as the prelude to a nationwide reversion to the values of the great Revolution of 1789. In mid-March Paris was declared a Commune, with its own revolutionary council denying the authority of the national government. Fighting broke out in Paris between Communards and members of the National Guard, many of whom joined the rebels. Countless atrocities were committed. Executions were carried out on public figures held to be hostile to the Commune; public buildings and monuments were destroyed as the conflict intensified. At last the government, recently returned to Versailles from Bordeaux, sent troops into the city to restore order, and the period of the Commune came to an end on 28 May 1871. In the battle to retake the city, it is estimated that the invading troops lost less than a thousand men, while the defenders lost at least 20,000. The whole affair, war and civil war combined, had not lasted a year from start to finish, but its effect would be very far-reaching.

COMMON KNOWLEDGE AND HINDSIGHT

By 1879, when Maupassant looked back at this troubled period to compose his story on the Franco-Prussian war, he had the benefit of knowing the outcome of events. He knew that France had lost Alsace-Lorraine, and that the Prussians had remained in eastern France until the last of the indemnity payments was made. He was also aware that the Republic formed in time of war had survived in spite of the opposition of the united royalist parties, whatever old scores still lay unsettled beneath the surface. Neither the Bourbons nor the Orleans dynasty had been restored to power, and by the time of his writing *Boule de Suif* in 1879, the house of Bonaparte had no direct heir to Napoléon III, as the Prince Impérial, son of Napoléon III and focus of the hopes of the pro-royalist travellers in *Boule de Suif*, was dead, killed that same year by tribesmen in South Africa. Napoléon III himself had died in 1873, broken in health, finally succumbing to the kidney disease from which he had suffered so painfully in the last years of his reign. Protected by his fellow monarch, Queen Victoria, he had spent his last days at Chislehurst in Kent with his Empress Eugénie, who outlived him into the twentieth century and presided over the erection of the Imperial mausoleum at Farnborough Abbey in Hampshire which is still a place of pilgrimage for supporters of the French royal family.

After the conservative presidency of MacMahon (1873-79), the more radical Jules Grévy (1879-87) brought in secularising reforms, for instance those concerning obligatory, non-denominational and free education, to strengthen the republican cause. Maupassant lived to see continuing battles of policy between state and church, but in the years between the end of the war and the publication of *Boule de Suif*, he saw the gradual imposition of republican values.

5

His story shows partisans of each of the political groupings: the Orleanists, in the count and his wife; a Bonapartist in Boule de Suif (symbolically attached to a lost cause, whereas Carré-Lamadon is ready to profit from whichever side is in power); and a republican in Cornudet, who uses the title "citizen / citizeness" as in the days of the Revolution, dreaming of glory to come when the world will be put to rights and monarchy will be abolished, and singing the revolutionary anthem (officially banned under the Second Empire, until its last few weeks). None of the political attachments of the characters, it seems, is alone sufficient to save the nation. The conversion needed is one of widespread moral enlightenment. The two nuns, representatives of spiritual priorities, are not committed to the political salvation of France. Their task is to save the bodies of the wounded, not to transform the situation which caused their injuries.

There had been two battles fought on French soil. One was the struggle to repel the invader, the other a civil war. *Boule de Suif* contains elements of both those conflicts.

THE INVASION OF NORMANDY

The Franco-Prussian War was recorded in the fullest detail, covered by journalists, drawn, photographed, described and explained by participants and spectators. Interpretation of events may lead to different conclusions according to whether the presentation is German or French, or whether an English reporter is pro-French or pro-German; some bias is inevitable. But on the question of the invasion of Normandy there was no doubt. The contemporary historians are unanimous in describing the speed with which the Prussian army, under General von Manteuffel, was able to move westwards across Normandy, meeting relatively little resistance.

In Picardy, General von Manteuffel's army had captured the city of Amiens on 28 November. There had been fierce fighting in defence of the city, but when the garrison within its walls finally surrendered and the Germans entered the city, it became clear that the main body of the Army of the North commanded by General Faidherbe had already moved away. The Prefect of the Somme had also departed, this after encouraging the citizens to remain calm and informing them that the army had retreated and that the National Guard had laid down its arms.

A report sent to *The Times* describes in resigned tones the events that followed, and their similarity to what is described in the opening sequence of *Boule de Suif* is unmistakable:

> The *rappel* began to beat at half-past three on the morning of the 28th., and from that hour till six there was a general *sauve qui peut* , the railway being retained for the military. [...] Then someone rushed in breathlessly to tell me that the inevitable two Uhlans were to be seen, and, as most of the people were very frightened, and some very angry, I began to fear difficulty in getting away. [...] At last the Prussians did come. Not two Uhlans, but an officer riding in advance of twelve men. Then more cavalry and infantry, which filled the Place Périgord, and massed themselves near the cathedral.

So much, then, for the hopes of those besieged in Paris, relying on the combined forces of the Army of the North and the Army of the Loire to force the German armies away from the capital. To the news of the fall of Amiens in the north was added the loss of Orléans in the south, after a brave struggle to reclaim it from the invaders. The apparently invincible Prussians continued to move west into Normandy, and the next great city to fall was Rouen, the capital of the province, where Maupassant had attended college and where he had been stationed with the army during the war.

Called into the army at the outbreak of war, Maupassant was in Normandy during the invasion, able to follow closely the progress of the enemy across his native land, and sharing in the defeat as the Army of the North was led westwards to avoid capture before the final surrender. Two surviving letters to his mother from his period of army service give some hint of his feelings at this time. He writes that he was nearly captured during the invasion of Normandy, but that his strong legs saved him. Even so, he had covered 'quinze lieues' (60 km) in one night 'avec notre armée en déroute.' Later he was in Paris, prepared for the bombardment and hoping that he would not have to stay in the barracks at Vincennes, partly because the old fortress seemed a likely target for Prussian cannons, partly because 'la vie de caserne est bien ennuyeuse.' Released from the army in November 1871, he went into the civil service in Paris, where he met Emile Zola and his circle and eventually launched his own career as a writer. The pessimistic view of the conduct of the war and the distrust of his fellow-countrymen which are expressed in *Boule de Suif* derive directly from Maupassant's own experiences.

THE CAPTURE OF ROUEN

Rouen was captured without a fight. On 4 December, the Prussians had fallen upon a detachment of French troops sent to watch German movements, and in the ensuing skirmish the French were driven back. This disheartening episode apparently decided the French commander, General Briand, to withdraw without further combat, so that on 5 December part of General von Manteuffel's army, under the command of General von Goeben, entered the city without opposition. Whatever the feelings of those citizens who believed they had been betrayed to the Germans, they had to submit to the demands of the forces of occupation for provisions and accommodation throughout the harsh winter; for the Germans used Rouen as a base for their winter quarters, confident enough to leave it in order to conduct their campaign towards Dieppe, which was captured in its turn. Of the towns north of the Seine, only Le Havre resisted the German attack, and remained open for sea traffic: hence the determination of the travellers in the story to reach Le Havre in order to sail for England .

In practical terms, the collapse of Normandy, with its rich supplies and good communications—the Prussians sank shipping in the Seine near Rouen to prevent use of the port—meant that the French Army of the North had to retrace its path in a wide arc, endeavouring to move past the German forces and close in on Paris. But General von Goeben was able to intercept them, and the French losses effectively signalled the end of their hopes, as intense cold and lack of provisions were to take their toll in the winter of 1870-71.

As for Rouen itself, the loss of the city caused general surprise, as well as concern. Amiens had at least been defended, whereas it seemed the army had simply walked away from Rouen, heading for the safety of Le Havre. However sensible this behaviour was, it did not appear well at the time, and the loss of the city without the striking of a single blow produced mournful reports all over Europe. On the day after Rouen fell, *The Times* produced an epic lament:

> The grand old Norman city—the home of the soundest and most enterprising population of France—one of the richest in glorious old traditions, in medieval monuments—one of the most conspicuous in modern industrial achievements—the city of WILLIAM THE CONQUEROR, of ST OUEN and M. POUYER-QUERTIER—Rouen has fallen!

In the nineteenth century, Rouen was a byword for prosperity. Maupassant shows this aspect of the city clearly, with his portrait of comfortable businessmen, more concerned about their profits than their country, and whose pursuits typify the area: Carré-Lamadon, the cotton baron, is exemplary in this respect. Rouen was renowned for all aspects of textile manufacture, still carried on there today, and Maupassant's ironic reference to a 'Rouennais pur sang', for whom snowflakes are an irresistible reminder of cotton, indicates the importance of the connection.

The words *marchand* , *commerçant* and *commis* are derogatory terms here, for at a time when other qualities are needed business acumen prevails, turning the citizens of Rouen into cowards. Caution is their watchword. The good bourgeois hide away the uniforms they were once pleased to wear, and are careful to avoid any appearance of aggression, 'émasculés par le commerce'(p. 51) as they are. Trade has become a kind of addiction; in the terms of the story it is a vice, which permits the well-off travellers to bargain with their sense of decency in order to protect their wealth. The leaders of their fighting men are 'guerriers de circonstance' in appearance only. Their characters are still founded in trade. The narrator refers to them as 'ex-marchands de suif ou de savon'(p. 50), purveyors of humble if necessary commodities, the first of which suggests the bargain which lies at the heart of the story of Boule de Suif herself. Loiseau has had no scruples in selling poor

9

wine to the army, and looks forward to collecting his money when all around him his country is in ruins. His whole business is built on someone else's misfortune, and yet his greed is acceptable in a society where profit is equated with personal worth. Everyone knows he is a scoundrel, but for his compatriots he is 'un vrai Normand', as if this excused his double dealing. The caricatural portrait of Loiseau's wife shows the degrading effect of overconcern with money; she has turned into a calculating machine, 'l'ordre et l'arithmétique de la maison de commerce'(p. 57).

For those who stay behind in the occupied city, the same rationale applies. Once the initial fear of atrocities has died down, life, which means business, goes on: 'le besoin du négoce travailla de nouveau le cœur des commerçants du pays'(p. 54). There is also the consideration that it would be better to coexist peacefully with the occupying forces than provoke retaliation. The majority of the citizens of Rouen find that they are able to carry out their obligations towards the invaders: 'Le devoir commençait pour les vaincus de se montrer gracieux envers les vainqueurs'(p. 52). The mentality of trade reasserts itself as they calculate the cost of feeding the soldiers billeted upon them.The narrator describes how Prussian officers might join the family for meals, appeasing their hosts by apologetic reference to the war. In return, the hosts do their best to be welcoming, inspired by the ulterior motive that it may be useful to have a friend on the winning side:

> ... puis on pouvait, un jour ou l'autre, avoir besoin de sa protection. En le ménageant on obtiendrait peut-être quelques hommes de moins à nourrir. Et pourquoi blesser quelqu'un dont on dépendait tout à fait ? (p. 52)

In this somewhat sarcastic mimicry of their thought processes, the narrator points to the pretext with which the citizens attempt to disguise their spineless behaviour. They have replaced the ancient virtues of their once warlike race, with the urbane politeness which they now esteem more highly than courage. A mordant contrast is made between the heroic past of Rouen and the pusillanimous behaviour of his contemporaries: 'Et la témérité n'est plus un défaut des bourgeois de Rouen, comme au temps des défenses héroïques de leur cité'(pp. 52-3).

It is not the army's departure from Rouen which is called into question in *Boule de Suif* , but the decadence of its citizens, the worthlessness of the degraded form of its "freedom", the reduction of the city's pride to a market where everything has its price. In the end, the defence of Normandy is left to a prostitute. Rouen was, after all, the city where Joan of Arc, symbol of a free and independent France, was handed over to the enemy with the connivance of her own people. Is Boule de Suif the only Joan of Arc the Second Empire could deserve?

REALITY AND FICTION

There is a great deal in *Boule de Suif* which would have had more meaning for Maupassant's contemporaries than it does for the modern reader. The editor, as the helpful edition of *Boule de Suif* by W.M. Landers shows, must demystify for the reader those references made by the author to things that were everyday knowledge in the Second Empire. Otherwise we shall not understand that the French army was composed of men conscripted on an unfair system of national ballot, permitting a man who did not wish to take up his place to buy his way out by paying another to replace him for a seven-year period of service. We are unfamiliar with the colour of the uniforms, so do not react knowledgeably to the information that some men have red trousers or that those who are 'sombres' must be artillerymen in grey. The idea of the Garde Nationale is only partly explained by references to the Home Guard or "Dad's Army"; nor perhaps will we understand the reference to 'francs-tireurs', not recognised as regular troops by the enemy and liable to be shot out of hand. The very journey itself that the travellers make holds a mystery for the present-day reader, who may wonder why the snowbound Rouennais did not take a train direct to Le Havre, instead of striking off across country to Dieppe in a horse-drawn carriage. The answer is, of course, that since the arrival of the Germans the rail service had been suspended and the entrance to Le Havre by land was blocked, but Maupassant does not mention these facts.

There are other things he chose to omit, not because they were too well known to bear repetition, but because they were not relevant to the point of his story, and it is interesting to see that he passes over any mention of the attractions of Rouen (of which he could write movingly on occasion) or any material description of the Hôtel du Cygne at Tôtes which served as the model for the Hôtel du Commerce where the travellers stay. In more recent times, its owners have publicised the picturesqueness of its rooms, especially the old kitchen hung with pots and pans, but the narrator merely notes that it was 'vaste' and overlooks its Norman cosiness.

What exactly his contemporaries made of the characters in the tale must have depended on how well they knew the inhabitants of Rouen. For some at least, rumour must have persuaded them to recognise in the heroine the robust figure of Adrienne-Annonciade Legay, 'Reine de la Cascade'. Maupassant's eye for significant detail may have drawn him to the true story of a music-hall performer on her way to visit a lover in Le Havre, but he omits her domestic arrangements and gives her a more heroic reason for leaving Rouen.

The portrait of 'Cornudet le démoc' was known to represent Maupassant's uncle by marriage, Charles Cord'homme, who told him the story of Adrienne Legay's encounter with a Prussian, but was not himself involved in the journey. He was, however, noted for his republican sympathies, as well as his abundant beard. The distinguished figure of the cotton baron Carré-Lamadon seemed to offer the characteristics, if not the all too easily recognizable appearance, of the industrialist Auguste-Thomas Pouyer-Quertier (named in the quotation from *The Times* on the fall of Rouen). He had made his money in cotton, and went on to be an important figure in French politics. But by 1872 he had had to resign from the government after a financial scandal. Anyone who recognized this possible model for Carré-Lamadon would have had the satisfaction of knowing that he had not prospered after all. Perhaps it was this kind of identification, as well as the criticism of the inhabitants of Rouen in general, which prompted Maupassant to write to Flaubert that, once the story was published: 'Je serai désormais obligé d'avoir des pistolets dans mes poches pour traverser Rouen'(quoted in *Etudes, Chroniques et Correspondance* , p. 272).

There was more information, however, that Maupassant and his contemporaries must have known or suspected, but which he does not mention specifically at all. With his personal experience plus his presence in Normandy at the time of the invasion, Maupassant cannot fail to have heard of, and discussed, perhaps with his old friend Flaubert, the scandal that besmirched the last hours in Rouen before it surrendered. Some said that the firing near the town-hall was due to rowdy elements, perhaps 'les rouges' (radicals) attempting to stage a coup. Was it children playing with jettisoned firearms (too heavy to run away with), as at Amiens ? Some declared it was a detachment of the guard who had mutinied on being told to throw down their arms, a rumour picked up by *The Times* . There were reports of German spies, secret deals with the enemy in the town hall itself, even scenes where armed insurrectionists threatened members of the town council. The scandal was sufficiently great to provoke enquiries and denials in newspapers at the time. The difference between what there was to know and what everybody thought may not have been substantial, but the uneasy sense of betrayal in high places was strong, and it is certainly that above all which Maupassant seeks to convey.

From the defeated Emperor in exile, the retreating army, the divided society characterised by the travellers in the coach, to their act of collaboration with the enemy, the same message is expressed: France, prostitute though she may be, deserves better treatment at the hands of her selfish people. According to the narrator the majority prefer to pay their conquerors rather than fight them, but there are still a few prepared to risk their lives in acts of unsung heroism:

> Les vases du fleuve ensevelissaient ces vengeances obscures, sauvages et légitimes, héroïsmes inconnus, attaques muettes, plus périlleuses que les batailles au grand jour et sans le retentissement de la gloire.(p. 53)

It is this unspoken element of the story which provided its inspiration. Maupassant's attitude to such heroism may be one of scepticism. The use of capitals in the sentence 'Car la haine de l'Etranger arme toujours quelques Intrépides prêts à mourir pour une Idée'(p. 53) suggests an ironic reluctance to believe that such ideals exist. Nevertheless, the event that is to be recounted in the story of Boule de Suif's action of self-sacrifice for the common good is as nearly heroic an act as the author's pessimistic view of mankind would allow him to contemplate.

THE FRANCO-PRUSSIAN WAR IN LATER WRITINGS

It is not possible here to do justice to the variety of stories subsequently composed by Maupassant on the subject of the war, but there are themes running through them which show the consistency of the author's thoughts on the subject, and his preoccupation with the moral decay of his own people.

Maupassant never wrote about particular battles or campaigns; typically he picks out incidents, almost 'faits divers', usually concerning civilians. Heroic prostitutes reappear in *Mlle Fifi* (1882) and in *Le Lit 29* (1884), both stories being set in and around Rouen. *Mlle Fifi* , the nickname of an effeminate and sadistic Prussian officer, relates the barbaric behaviour of a company of Prussian troops in an occupied chateau. 'Mlle Fifi' himself is determined to abuse and humiliate the prostitute Rachel and her companions brought out from Rouen to entertain them, but Rachel at least shows that she has the courage to retaliate when her country is insulted, declaring that to sleep with prostitutes is not to triumph over *French* women, and fortuitously stabbing him to death with a dessert knife.

The notion of the heroic prostitute who is not so degraded that she cannot avenge an attack on her country is differently developed in *Le Lit 29*. The basis for this story is already contained in *Boule de Suif*, when the travellers attempt to persuade the prostitute to sleep with the officer by recalling examples of women who sacrificed their bodies for some noble cause:

> On parla même en termes voilés de cette Anglaise de grande famille qui s'était laissé inoculer une horrible et contagieuse maladie pour la transmettre à Bonaparte... (p. 80)

In this version, the heroine is a prostitute who, having contracted a venereal disease from the enemy, refuses medical treatment. Instead she uses her disease as a weapon against her Prussian customers, until her health gives

14

way and she is condemned to a miserable death in bed 29 in the hospital, where a former lover from the French army is ashamed to be seen visiting her. Her pathetic eagerness to see her old flame, now decorated for his bravery, turns to bitterness as she realises that she is despised, and provokes the final outburst which is the point of the story. The dying woman expresses the criticism that is the theme of many of Maupassant's war stories: that those who are acclaimed for their courage and rewarded by society have not necessarily achieved as much as their more humble compatriots, whose deeds go unrecorded.

The siege of Paris forms the background to *Deux Amis* (1883), but the majority of stories show scenes from Normandy, focusing on the preoccupations of country people or peasants, whose concern, like that of Madame Follenvie in *Boule de Suif*, is not for politics or ideals, but for the humble lives of those who must work for a living. In stories such as these, the author investigates the motivations of patriotism, and his ironic vision fixes upon the essential selfishness of human activities. In *Saint-Antoine* (1883), the peasant farmer whose nickname forms the title of the story boasts that he is not afraid of the Prussians, but in reality his courage is based on the belief that they will not come to his village. When, like the rest, he is given a Prussian soldier to feed, he vents his fury by feeding "his" German as if he were a pig to be fattened. Although this is interpreted by the other villagers and Germans as hearty friendliness, it is in fact an act of aggression. Unable to attack the enemy in military fashion, Saint-Antoine takes a peasant's revenge on his victim, turning him into an object of ridicule and thereby regaining his own sense of superiority. His victim is finally provoked and they fight, leaving the farmer with no alternative but to kill his "guest" and hide the body under the dunghill. Once the danger is over, his Norman cunning enables him to ingratiate himself once more with the occupying force, to the extent that another man is punished for his deed.

In *Le Père Milon* (1883) and *La Mère Sauvage* (1884), the invader is not hated because of some sense of national injury. Père Milon has murdered a number of Prussians while looking after others who are billeted in his home. When his offence is discovered, it is difficult for the Prussian colonel to believe this confession of murder from such an old man. His explanation reveals a personal attitude towards the enemy rather than a political or patriotic one:

> ... c'est vous qu'avez tué mon pére, qu'était soldat de l'Empereur premier. Sans compter que vous avez tué mon fils cadet, François, le mois dernier, auprès d'Evreux. Je vous en devais, j'ai payé. Je sommes quittes. (*Le Père Milon* , in *'Boule de Suif' et autres contes normands* , p. 225)

In *La Mère Sauvage* , the strong, silent peasant woman looks after the four young Germans billeted on her, establishing an almost maternal relationship with them. The narrator of the story makes the observation that the poor cannot afford to be patriotic:

> Les humbles, ceux qui paient le plus parce qu'ils sont pauvres et que toute charge nouvelle les accable, ceux qu'on tue par masses, qui forment la vraie chair à canon, parce qu'ils sont le nombre, ceux qui souffrent enfin le plus cruellement des atroces misères de la guerre, parce qu'ils sont les plus faibles et les moins résistants, ne comprennent guère ces ardeurs belliqueuses, ce point d'honneur excitable et ces prétendues combinaisons politiques qui épuisent en six mois deux nations, la victorieuse comme la vaincue. (*La Mère Sauvage* , op.cit., p. 342)

On the day that she hears her son has been killed in the war, this mother is capable of killing her German "sons" in cold-blooded retaliation.

In other stories, such as *Un Coup d'Etat* (1884), *Les Prisonniers* (1884) and *Les Rois* (1887), the emphasis lies upon the gratuitousness of events. In these examples, it is the French who are the objects of Maupassant's ironic humour. The range of material shows a variety of attitudes on both sides in the struggle. *L'Aventure de Walter Schnaffs* (1883) expresses sympathy with the peace-loving, homesick German trooper who takes refuge in imprisonment as an escape from fighting, while his boastful captors glory in the triumph of having overcome his supposed resistance. In *Deux Amis* (1883), it is the turn of two Parisian anglers lured by the forbidden pleasures of the Seine to display patriotic solidarity when faced with death at the hands of the enemy

No-one is allowed to have the monopoly of bravery or privilege. The different uniforms cannot disguise the essential human vices and virtues shared by all, nor is the wearing of a uniform seen as a justification for inhumanity. For the inhabitants of a beleaguered land, the abuses inflicted by an occupying force may be indistinguishable from those previously committed by the home forces. All Maupassant's writings depict selfishness; war, like any theatre of human passions, allows us to view the unpleasantly appetitive disposition of mankind.

Chapter Two

The Creation of *Boule de Suif*

Maupassant's first short story, *La Main d'Ecorché* , was published in 1875, while he was employed in the civil service. Of the handful which he is known to have written between 1875 and 1880, when *Boule de Suif* appeared in the collection *Les Soirées de Médan* , only one seems to have any direct bearing on *Boule de Suif* . This is *Le Mariage du Lieutenant Laré* (1877), which has as its setting the winter of 1870-71 and relates an adventure in which a young girl is saved by the lieutenant of the title. Apart from the snow-covered landscape which is the setting for the romance and which inspired Maupassant to compose the remarkable description of falling snow, 'plutôt sensation que bruit', incorporated in a reorganised form into *Boule de Suif* , the story is not memorable. Perhaps the author was not satisfied with it himself, for he later reworked it under the title of *Les Idées du Colonel* (1884).

The creation of *Boule de Suif* is quite well documented, since the author mentions it in his letters to his friend and adviser, Gustave Flaubert. Their correspondence gives an intriguing picture of Maupassant's attitude to his work. Emile Zola had invited him to contribute to a collection of stories set at the time of the Franco-Prussian War, and Maupassant refers to this in a letter to Flaubert as 'notre volume de nouvelles'. He was already aware of the contents of some of the other stories, and confides to his friend that it was Zola's idea to publish his own *L'Attaque du Moulin* together with *Sac au dos,* by J.-K. Huysmans, and *La Saignée* , by Henry Céard. According to Maupassant, Zola thought that it would make 'un curieux volume, peu chauvin, et d'une note particulière.' Zola had then invited Léon Hennique, Paul Alexis and Maupassant himself to contribute a story each. The other writers hoped that the already established name of Zola would help to sell the collection.

The young man continues this letter of 5 January 1880 by explaining the aim of the assembled writers in publishing the book. He insists that they do not wish in any way to be unpatriotic, or express any single viewpoint. They just want to show the war as it was. But ultimately Maupassant did have the intention of attacking conventional attitudes, as he reveals to Flaubert that the stories will show the military as 'des êtres médiocres comme les autres', whose activities result in the deaths of their men 'par simple stupidité'. According to Maupassant, each writer's unbiased version will inevitably annoy the bourgeoisie, which seems to suggest that he himself associated bourgeois society with a certain kind of jingoistic patriotism. His disapproval of his compatriots' behaviour would be expressed in his own contribution too, for he tells Flaubert that his story will be a source of annoyance to the inhabitants of Rouen, and yet is not as critical of them as it might have been.

In March he was writing again to his friend, this time asking him to read the proofs of his story, but not to ask him to change too much, as the number of lines was already settled. He was, though, quite prepared to substitute one word for another, as 'l'épithète est une chose grave qui peut toujours être modifiée.'

By the end of April, the collection of stories had appeared, and Maupassant could write once more to Flaubert, to describe the success of his contribution. Flaubert had already praised *Boule de Suif* , and Maupassant was glad to tell his friend that other writers had done the same, assuring him that the story would enjoy lasting popularity. Clearly Maupassant felt sufficiently encouraged by its success to believe that *Des Vers* , his new volume of poems, would profit by his improved status as a writer.

MAUPASSANT AND NATURALISM

Complaining about the newspaper reviews of *Les Soirées de Médan* , Maupassant refers to the ideas of the naturalist school of writing. His attachment to the group of writers who met in Zola's house at Médan, and enjoyed his undoubted hospitality as well as sharing in his views, was sincere, and Maupassant continued to respect Zola's opinion, although he was not such an unconditional disciple as Paul Alexis, who devotedly followed and defended Zola's naturalist principles, and later took his side in the Dreyfus affair.

Like his mentor Flaubert, Maupassant was an independent. His association with Zola's group was brief, for he was unable to subscribe wholeheartedly to the scientific pretensions to the representation of man in society which that view entailed. The documentary approach, with its doctrine of strict observation and impassivity on the part of the author, which was the ideal of the naturalist school (although few, least of all Zola himself, succeeded in sustaining the "experimental" method of writing) can be seen in the *Soirées de Médan* , which appeared to some critics as a naturalist manifesto.

In a favourable review of the collection, Edouard Rod refers to the hostility the book will provoke:

> L'union de ces jeunes écrivains montre la force; sans aucun doute elle inquiétera les adversaires passionnés du naturalisme... Ceux qui, au contraire, s'intéressent au mouvement moderne salueront avec plaisir leur œuvre collective toute pleine de promesses et déjà de réalisations.
>
> (In *Boule de Suif* , Conard ed., p. 127)

In particular, the attempt to write in a documentary fashion induced authors to depict aspects of society which had not previously been considered suitable for literature, such as the lives of working-class people, criminals or social outcasts. It followed that realist and, later, naturalist writing was associated with a certain spirit of revolution, implicitly protesting against the conditions depicted in their works. Zola's *Rougon-Macquart* cycle studied the lives and generations of whole families. The depiction of working conditions, the exposure of the materialism of the Second Empire and the cynicism of the ruling classes brought him into conflict with the authorities for his outspokenness. Since the label "naturalist" was associated with the idea of criticism of social injustices, it is not surprising that some reviewers of *Les Soirées de Médan* saw the same disparagement of bourgeois values which they had recognised in Zola's earlier writing. An extract from a review of *Les*

Soirées de Médan by the hostile Léon Chapron, writing in *L'Evénement*, shows the association between the style of writing and the idea of social reform which the writing had come to represent.

> Eh bien, pathologie ou non, nous voudrions bien qu'on ne trouvât plus d'éternelles excuses pour les assassins, les nymphomanes, les joueurs et—surtout—pour les naturalistes.
>
> (op.cit., p.126)

The spirit of Zola's crusade to break down barriers of inertia attracted other artists to him, so the assimilation of like-minded men to a "school" of naturalist writing was inevitable, if not accurate.

In the case of the *Soirées de Médan*, with all its attendant publicity (to which Maupassant was an enthusiastic contributor, as shown by his article 'Comment ce livre a été fait' for *Le Gaulois*, 17 April 1880), the cause of naturalism alone was not enough. Another reason for the unity of the six authors who wrote stories for the collection was not simply a wish to participate in a literary exercise, or even to irritate the bourgeois citizens of France, but the chance to express their shared experience—the defeat of France by united German forces and France's surrender in 1871.

It may be of interest here to provide some comment on the stories in the collection, both as an indication of their authors' part in the Franco-Prussian war and for comparison with *Boule de Suif*, which was printed second in the collection, after Zola's story.

LES SOIREES DE MEDAN

EMILE ZOLA (1840-1902) : *L'ATTAQUE DU MOULIN*

In 1870, Emile Zola was working on the first stages of his *Rougon-Macquart* cycle. The abdication of the Emperor in September was a vindication of Zola's republican sympathies, but as the war continued, Zola took his wife from Paris to the relative safety of Marseilles. Unable to return to Paris because of the siege, he then went to offer his services to the republican administration in Bordeaux, later moving with them when they transferred to Versailles, and writing reports of the meetings of the Assemblée Nationale for the newspaper *La Cloche* .

His preface to the stories is a challenge, inviting the criticism which the collection in fact received from the opponents of naturalism and all it stood for. Given here in its entirety, it shows that Zola had in mind more than a demonstration of the techniques of naturalistic writing, but rather a spirit of solidarity among the authors.

> Les nouvelles qui suivent ont été publiées, les unes en France, les autres à l'étranger. Elles nous ont paru procéder d'une idée unique, avoir une même philosophie: nous les réunissons.
>
> Nous nous attendons à toutes les attaques, à la mauvaise foi et à l'ignorance dont la critique courante nous a déjà donné tant de preuves. Notre seul souci a été d'affirmer publiquement nos véritables amitiés et, en même temps, nos tendances littéraires.

Médan, 1er mars 1880

(Les Soirées de Médan , Livre de Poche, p. 13)

L'Attaque du Moulin had already been published in Russia in 1877, and its story of a village Romeo and Juliet caught up in the follies of war did not appeal to Maupassant. It could just as well have been written by George Sand or Daudet, he confided to Flaubert in a letter dated by Dumesnil 'fin avril 1880' (*Etudes, chroniques et correspondance* , p. 286), from which the following comments on Huysmans, Céard, Hennique and Alexis are also taken. However, the romantic idyll of the opening section provides a forceful contrast with the subsequent description of the violence of French and German sides alike, exploding the myth of military glory. In the dramatic tableau which closes the tale, the demented heroine crouches by the corpses of her lover and her father in the smoking ruins of the mill. The French captain whose manoeuvres have largely contributed to the tragedy now salutes her with his sword. The tactlessness of his cry 'Victoire! Victoire!' underlines the emptiness of such a triumph. The battles take place in and around an old mill, which is almost the central character in the story . At first the setting for an innocent romance, it becomes the focus of an enemy onslaught. The miller,

22

his family and the mill are finally destroyed in a military test of strength which proves nothing.

Zola's gift for epic description would be more fully expressed in his novel *La Débâcle* (1892), which takes as its centrepiece the experiences of two young combattants in the disaster of the battle of Sedan and its sequel, ending with the Paris Commune.

JORIS-KARL HUYSMANS (1848-1907) : *SAC AU DOS*

This near-autobiographical account of the experiences of a reservist called up in 1870 shows the lack of organisation and discipline which characterised the French forces in the Franco-Prussian War. The antihero, Eugène Lejantel, falls ill before he reaches the front. He spends his war moving from one army hospital to another, until the ordeal is over and he can return to his comfortable flat in Paris. The flippant, self-debunking narrative indicates a "bad attitude" towards authority in the description of a series of events which create a convincing picture of his time as an invalid. Lejantel is both amused and disgusted by what he sees, and his story is designed to give insight into the realities of the war period. Legends of heroic sacrifice are dispelled in the description of drunken conscripts bawling the *Marseillaise* as the train for the camp at Châlons pulls out of the station. In the hospital, serious thoughts are inspired by the shock of seeing a real soldier suffering from injuries received in the battle of Froeschwiller. But selfishness always reasserts itself in the struggle for survival. Lejantel's world is reduced to the contents of his kitbag, which is constantly shouldered as the order comes to move on. The use of the first person and the humour of the narration give this story liveliness.

Maupassant's laconic assessment of the story—'Pas fameux. Pas de sujet, pas de composition, peu de style'—seems strangely myopic, and perhaps indicates his real distance from the naturalists.

HENRY CEARD (1851-1924) : *LA SAIGNEE*

Céard's war story reflects his experience as a member of the forces called upon to defend Paris, its opening lines taking the reader straight to the heart of the matter: 'Dix heures du matin, un jour de la fin d'octobre, à Paris, pendant le siège.' The author's choice of time and place is the setting for the people's dissatisfaction with the management of the war and the inactivity of the military within besieged Paris. Crowds assembled outside the Hôtel de Ville clamour for action, while the authorities within deliberate. The blood-letting in the title refers to the unsuccessful sortie which is eventually ordered by the general. The evocation of Paris under siege is accompanied by the adventures of the general's mistress, once a favourite at court in the Second Empire. Through her experiences, the misery of life in occupied Versailles is related, and eventually Versailles and Paris are brought together as the general and his mistress are reunited, with tragic consequences. The story relies heavily for its effect on the contrast between the harshness of the soldiers' lives, thrown away to protect the reputation of their leaders, and the self-indulgence of the general and his mistress.

Maupassant's judgement, 'lourd, très lourd, pas vraisemblable, des tics de style, mais des choses fines et curieuses', indicates perhaps the imbalance between the documentary aspect of the story and its unconvincing romance.

LEON HENNIQUE (1851-1935) : *L'AFFAIRE DU GRAND 7*

Hennique came to France from Guadeloupe to study law, but his studies were interrupted when he joined the artillery in 1870, and his story contains much reference to guns and shooting, since it tells of an incident when drunken soldiers go on the rampage after one of their number is shot in the local brothel. The injured man makes his way back to the barracks, only to die before help can be given. His comrades are bewildered and angry. In their determination to exact revenge for the death of their comrade, they set out to punish the owner of the brothel, whom they hold responsible. The officers

24

lose control of their men, who avenge themselves by murdering the innocent and helpless prostitutes, while the enemy draws gradually nearer. A climax is reached when they kill one of their officers, who has dared to criticise their behaviour. The conclusion shows the officers meeting to discuss how to deal with this outrage, and the final lines are spoken by their chief, whose cynical judgement underlines the futility of it all:

> —Vous ne savez pas? dit-il... Eh bien! laissons passer une huitaine de jours, vous verrez qui regrettera l'affaire de cette nuit... Plus bêtes que des enfants tous ces clampins-là !... Ils ont brisé leur joujou.(op.cit., p. 245)

Hennique's story of frustration and injustice drew some praise from Maupassant: 'bien, bonne patte d'écrivain, quelque confusion par places.'

PAUL ALEXIS (1847-1901) : *APRES LA BATAILLE*

This last story of the collection narrates, as the title suggests, events outside the fighting. An infantryman is following a road away from the battleground when he has the good fortune to be given a lift by a woman driving a wagon. She has been to search for her husband's body, and is now carrying his coffin home for burial in his native Brittany. At first unwilling to take a passenger, the young woman has pity on the soldier, who collapses exhausted by the side of the coffin. During the course of their journey together, the two travellers discover that they have more in common than their social background and *mores* would suggest.

The story begins with the soldier's confused memory of the battle, the only one he has ever seen and which for him was soon over. His impatience to fight after four wretched months of training in the camps rapidly gives way to fear and confusion, as he lies in a field of beetroot trying to protect his head with the butt of his rifle. The futility of the exercise upon which he is engaged, and in which so many of his comrades lose their lives, is made more apparent when, dragging himself away from the battle with an injured foot, the soldier's best hope is that he will be found by a passer-by, even a

Prussian. With the arrival of the Baronne de Plémoran in answer to the soldier's prayers, the author chooses to focus upon the chance encounter of two strangers, transformed by the roles forced upon them by circumstances.

Maupassant had a poor opinion of this story and his comment to Flaubert, considering it no more than a pale imitation of the more provocative Barbey d'Aurevilly, was dismissive.

A RETROSPECTIVE VIEW

Although the six stories have a common theme, their authors did not remain united. Maupassant's sympathy for Emile Zola endured, as he showed in an article on him, written for *La Revue Bleue* in 1883, where he discusses Zola's definition of naturalism ('un coin de la nature vu à travers un tempérament'), but adds his own gloss in an attempt to reconcile the differences between them:

> Car la vérité absolue, la vérité sèche, n'existe pas, personne ne pouvant avoir la prétention d'être un miroir parfait. [...] Toutes ces querelles littéraires sont donc surtout des querelles de tempérament; et on érige le plus souvent en questions d'école, en questions de doctrine, les tendances diverses des esprits.
> (In *Etudes, Chroniques et Correspondance* , p. 82)

Huysmans would go further in his separation from Zola, describing Zola's naturalism as materialism, and urging other writers to look beyond that level to a higher, more spiritual naturalism, as he did himself. His novel *A Rebours,* published in 1884, had been a revelation of the "decadent" attitude which came to be characteristic of late nineteenth-century art and marked a turning away from the social realism of Zola's naturalism. Composing a preface for his novel in 1904, Huysmans looked back twenty years, and acknowledged the achievement of the naturalist "school" even as he criticised it:

> On était alors en plein naturalisme; mais cette école, qui devait rendre l'inoubliable service de situer des personnages réels dans des milieux exacts, était condamnée à se rabâcher, en piétinant sur place.

Henry Céard's concern for accuracy was so great that he eventually became disillusioned with Zola's unscientific lack of objectivity. He had lent a copy of Claude Bernard's *Introduction à l'étude de la médecine expérimentale* to Zola in order to help him formulate his ideas. When Zola failed to see that the argument he was using in his *Le Roman Expérimental* to support his thesis of the novel as a work of scientific observation was untenable, Céard's disappointment was intense. It was not possible for him to subscribe to the theories expressed, and so began the separation from Zola which was completed by the Dreyfus affair.

Only Paul Alexis continued to follow the master and undertake to defend his literary principles. In 1891 he sent a telegram to the journalist Jules Huret, in response to his *Enquête sur l'Evolution littéraire* , which consisted of the plain statement: 'Naturalisme pas mort, lettre suit.' Later he would stand by Zola and support him in his defence of Dreyfus.

For Maupassant, the demise of naturalism was hastened by his growing confidence in his own more personal vision. It is doubtful that he was ever a naturalist in the sense understood and propagated by the Médan group, although he no doubt enjoyed their companionship as writers. The success of his contribution to the *Soirées de Médan* , however, set him on his meteoric path to fame, and he was soon writing his own observations on the nature of literature. With the death of Gustave Flaubert in 1880, Maupassant had lost his true kindred spirit. His subsequent writings show that he was in fact the disciple that the great novelist had affectionately seen in him.

In 1930, Léon Hennique, last survivor of the six, wrote a preface for a new edition of the *Soirées de Médan* that recaptured the excitement the young writers had felt in their fellowship of literary endeavour. Hennique expresses his nostalgia for the days of enthusiasm and mutual admiration as they prepared the collection of stories that would arouse the bourgeoisie.

> Le livre des six—Zola y avait ajouté une combative préface—est aux mains de son éditeur... On l'imprime... On le broche... on le dédicace... Il trône à la devanture des libraires... La critique est furieuse, attaque... Nous n'avons pas peur; nous nous amusons. Le public s'amuse aussi, achète. Temps simple! Temps probe, affectueux!
>
> (*Les Soirées de Médan* , Livre de Poche, p. 11)

Chapter Three

Structure and Narrative Technique in
Boule de Suif

TIME

On Monday 5 December 1870, the city of Rouen fell to German troops under the command of General von Manteuffel. From this historical episode, the events narrated in the story follow in chronological sequence, though not immediately. The narration describes the period of adjustment under the occupation, and it is 'au bout de quelque temps' (p. 52) that calm is restored. After the introduction, the description of a journey, its interruption and continuation, covers a six-day period.

Day One contains the journey to Tôtes, and the fateful encounter with a German officer. The author is precise about the details of the day, giving times and making calculations. It is half-past four in the morning of 'un mardi matin' when the travellers meet in the courtyard of the Hôtel de Normandie in Rouen to begin their journey, but by ten o'clock 'on n'avait pas fait quatre lieues.' Further references to the problems of driving a coach through deep snow are provided; the men get out when there is a slope, to lighten the load for the straining horses, of which we already know that there are six instead of the usual four; in spite of these precautions, the wheels are stuck in a drift, 'et il fallut deux heures pour la dégager.' The awareness of the passing of time is accentuated by the internal clock of the passengers' hunger. By one o'clock, they should have arrived at the half-way stop for lunch, and by three in the afternoon Boule de Suif can wait no longer and produces her basket of food. Night has fallen by the time they reach their projected lunch-time stop. Lights have to be lit on the coach, and the narrator is particularly emphatic about the duration of the journey, adding up the hours for the reader. The arithmetical calculation is admittedly rather approximate, but the point

28

concerning their privation is well taken nonetheless:

> On avait marché onze heures, ce qui, avec les deux heures de repos laissées en quatre fois aux chevaux pour manger l'avoine et souffler, faisait quatorze. (p. 65)

The aim is clearly to create an impression of urgency. This is a journey with a timetable, all the more pressing because it is also a bid to escape the clutches of an occupying force.

When the travellers are frustrated in their plan by the intervention of the officer at the Hôtel du Commerce, the precise time gradually becomes irrelevant, and fades from the narrative, to be replaced by a more fundamental calendar of meal times and sleep, occasionally enlivened by attempts to speed their departure.

The arrival at the hotel is described as a time of preparation for a meal and for the prospects of the journey to come, which the travellers intend to resume at a specific time: 'Comme on avait décidé qu'on partirait à huit heures le lendemain, tout le monde se trouva dans la cuisine'(p. 71). But the timetable begins to disintegrate, as they see their horseless, driverless carriage standing under its hood of snow in the yard. So the day that began with plans for departure gradually lapses into a kind of limbo, as the travellers find no reason for their detention.

At ten o'clock, there is the futile meeting with the landlord, followed by the frustrating interview with the officer which in turn leads nowhere. Condemned to await the officer's apparently capricious goodwill, the passengers begin the weary round of card-playing and conversation with which they attempt to kill the time over which they no longer have any control. Even when Boule de Suif resolves the mystery of their delay, her refusal to comply with the officer's request deprives her fellow-travellers of any means of action. From this point onwards the days pass in a sequence of meals and distractions, all characterised by frustration.

Day Two ends with the game of cards with the landlord, designed to extract from him useful information that will enable his companions to devise a plan of escape. There is no interest in the game of cards as such, and when it fails to produce the desired result, the other players call a halt.

From Day Three, the action moves episodically, as periods of boredom are broken by bids to put an end to captivity. Subjective reactions give colour to the narration of time passing, for we no longer experience it through our own knowledge of duration, but remodelled by the emotions of the captive travellers.

> On se leva encore d'assez bonne heure le lendemain avec un espoir indéterminé, un désir plus grand de s'en aller, une terreur du jour à passer dans cette horrible petite auberge. (p. 76)

A walk in the afternoon produces no results, only the knowledge that conditions are too bad for them to try to escape on foot. It occurs to them, though, that Tôtes may well be the place where a French sortie from Dieppe would confront the Prussian forces, and that they really ought to get away as soon as possible. The introduction of this new fear puts pressure on everybody to find a solution, thus heightening the tension, as they find themselves powerless. They would like to follow their own timetable of escape to Dieppe, which would restore their control over their own actions and permit them to continue their journey to safety. Until this happens they are condemned to pass the time like prisoners, and so their impatience with Boule de Suif increases.

Day Four starts as wearily as Day Three until, with the departure of Boule de Suif for the baptism, the other travellers see their chance to plot against her, 'car on sentait bien qu'à la fin il fallait décider quelque chose'(p. 78). After the refusal of their request to be allowed to leave without her, they join together to break down the prostitute's resistance to the officer. Tension increases as the plot is hatched, and reaches its climax in the unexpected contribution of the elderly nun.

Day Five contains elements of Day Three, with the afternoon walk that gives the count the opportunity to speak to Boule de Suif alone, and for the first time she is absent from the evening meal. This constitutes a break in what had become a pattern. The routine of captivity is at last interrupted, and is seen by the travellers as an indication of change. When they realise that their plan has worked, they rejoice in their renewed opportunity to proceed, and their hopes for the future are conveyed by a change of mood and pace as they

30

suddenly find everything around them interesting and delightful, whereas before it had gone unnoticed in the general sense of gloom:

> Le comte parut s'apercevoir que Mme. Carré-Lamadon était charmante, le manufacturier fit des compliments à la comtesse. La conversation fut vive, enjouée, pleine de traits. (p. 83)

In contrast to the inaction of the previous days, Day Six is animated, divided between the triumph of the travellers and the discomfiture of Boule de Suif.

Once aboard the coach, the passengers can renew their concern with their interrupted timetable. Time becomes manageable and measurable once more. 'Au bout de trois heures de route'(p. 87) it is time to eat, and the picnic which matches the meal of Day One can take place. It seems as if order and comfort have been restored until Cornudet, by whistling and singing the *Marseillaise* reminds the 'honnêtes gens autorisés'(p. 57) that by betraying a compatriot they have also betrayed France. Their 'bras vengeurs' have not been raised in combat, and this inescapable reminder of their cowardice effectively replaces the humiliations endured in the hotel by another form of tribulation which lengthens the hours of their journey, 'contraignant les esprits las et exaspérés à poursuivre le chant d'un bout à l'autre'(p. 89).

SPACE

If time is not what it seems to the harassed travellers on the road to Dieppe, then neither is space. Maupassant uses their enforced proximity—in the coach and in the hotel—as a means of exploiting their essential hostility towards one another but there is first of all the contrast of the group with their surroundings. Seen as a unit, the travelling party moves as one through the unwelcoming landscape, battling against the obstacle presented by the snow. Compared with the microcosm within the coach, the outdoors seems limitless. The falling snow which transformed their figures and turned them into shapeless bundles has imposed a similar disguise on the countryside, making it mysterious and unfriendly. The hostility of the weather is matched by the difficult times in which they live. The war has frozen all instincts of

31

hospitality or aid and the attempts to find food at nearby farms bring no
results:

> Les messieurs coururent aux provisions dans les fermes au bord
> du chemin, mais ils n'y trouvèrent pas même de pain, car le
> paysan, défiant, cachait ses réserves dans la crainte d'être pillé
> par les soldats qui, n'ayant rien à se mettre sous la dent, prenaient
> par force ce qu'ils découvraient. (p. 60)

The arrival at the hotel therefore sets up a focus of retreat from the hostile
outside world, and this will continue so throughout, even though the hotel
also becomes a prison, when the officer refuses them permission to leave.
The great kitchen of the hotel offers warmth and some hospitality. They take
their meals there, play cards or converse. The fire in the hearth attracts
Cornudet to settle there with his beer and pipe, where he represents an image
of retreat from the problems of the world outside. At the same time, the hotel
is 'cette horrible petite auberge', from which they would like to escape. In
fact, each time the travellers are confined within a space, it becomes a kind of
prison: first the coach, then the hotel and finally the coach again. The nature
of their imprisonment varies from physical restraint, as in their inability to
continue their journey until they have permission to do so, to the sense of
humiliation they must endure when found to be morally at fault. The fact that
these can occur in one and the same place helps to create the unresolved
tension on which the story rests.

There are three ventures into the world outside the inn: the first, when they
find that they cannot leave as they had planned. Naturally, the travellers wish
to move on, and so the search which leads them into the town is part of an
attempt to escape. The search for their coachman leads them into a world
turned upside down. The occupying force is engaged in humble domestic
chores, quite inappropriate for the role of conqueror. The local women are
giving the orders; even an 'aïeule tout impotente' (p. 71) is able to command.
The effect is rather as if the travellers had emerged from the reality of their
stay in the hotel into a surreal world where no-one does what is expected of
them, and their coachman is at last to be found 'dans le café du village,
attablé fraternellement avec l'ordonnance de l'officier'(p. 72). Astonished by
the spectacle of Prussian soldiers working for the villagers, the travellers are

'fort inquiets' as they return to the inn, where alone normal values are preserved.

The effect of alienation is continued when the party decide to take a walk on the third day of their stay, minus Cornudet, who prefers the fireside, and the nuns, who go to the church or the priest's house. In each of these cases, it is clear that a congenial refuge has been found, whereas the majority of the party go out simply because it is the only alternative to boredom, 'comme on s'ennuyait à périr.' In fact, conditions are so bad outside that they soon feel uncomfortable in the intense cold. Again, the landscape is devoid of features they can recognise:

> ...et, lorsque la campagne se découvrit, elle leur apparut si effroyablement lugubre sous cette blancheur illimitée que tout le monde aussitôt retourna, l'âme glacée et le cœur serré. (p. 77)

Moreover, they are obliged to recognise that they would be unable to escape through the snow. But there is another factor in their feeling of captivity, in the person of the officer himself. Maupassant places him like another obstacle, an ally of the bad weather, literally blocking their exit:

> Tout à coup, au bout de la rue, l'officier parut. Sur la neige qui fermait l'horizon, il profilait sa grande taille de guêpe en uniforme. (p. 77)

This reminder of their humiliation affects the rest of the day. They are not free to go anywhere, it seems, that does not recall their vulnerable state. They are constantly constrained by their surroundings and by the company. Not until Boule de Suif goes to church do the others feel free to make contact, and thus they are able to engage in the plot which definitively separates them from her. So that the afternoon walk which takes place on Day Five, has a motive which the earlier one had not. Consequently the author concentrates on the conversation engineered between Boule de Suif and the count, and there is no mention of the biting cold which had obliged them to turn back on Day Three.

It is Boule de Suif's absence on the last night which gives the rest a foretaste of freedom. 'Aussitôt un grand soupir de soulagement sortit de toutes les poitrines, une allégresse parut sur tous les visages'(p. 83), which they celebrate by drinking champagne and enjoying jokes at Boule de Suif's expense. Not even the more refined members of the party can resist the invitation to prurient laughter created by Loiseau's insinuations about noises overhead, or fail to share his pretended concern for Boule de Suif's treatment at the hands of the Prussian. As for Cornudet's denunciation of their infamy, given his personal attempt to effect a transaction with her it can be dismissed with hilarity as "sour grapes". This burst of conviviality heralds the departure on the following day; as the travellers board the coach again, they are 'radieux', with restored self-confidence now that they have escaped from their durance at the inn. In spite of the prostitute's obvious distress, their picnic on the journey is good-humoured enough. The return to the complacency which characterised the start of the venture shows that the majority of the travelling party feel that their period of detention and frustration is over. The description of the separate provisions of food for the meal en route indicates that the travellers are no longer operating as a unit, as they did when they were threatened by the presence of the German officer, but have now reverted to their individual preoccupations. It is an assertion of their separateness and a preparation for the parting to come. They have nothing to share any more and they take care to establish an appropriate distance between themselves and the prostitute, whom they no longer acknowledge.

Cornudet's revenge on the bourgeois takes away their feeling of liberation, and the final section of the story replaces the sense of freedom by a return to constraint:

> Toutes les figures se rembrunirent. Le chant populaire, assurément, ne plaisait point à ses voisins. Ils devinrent nerveux, agacés, et avaient l'air prêts à hurler comme des chiens qui entendent un orgue de barbarie.(pp. 88-9)

As the night closes in, the narrator's sight fades, distance is lost and the reader's impression of the coach is reduced to that of a dark interior in which are heard the disembodied sounds of the *Marseillaise* and a woman crying.

MOVEMENT

The adventure of the travellers must be set, of course, against the introduction to *Boule de Suif* , which not only provides the reason for the activities described but also paints the mood of desperation and urgency which characterises them. The retreat of the French army which opens the story is a prelude to the flight of the citizens from Rouen. The advance of the Prussian troops and their occupation of the city prefigures the smaller-scale domination of the travellers by a single officer, and in the same way in which the Germans control every aspect of life in the city, so the commandant oversees the movements of his hostages, preventing them from acting independently and frustrating their attempts to journey on.

Moreover, just as the invaders are able to impose their will upon the citizens by their mere presence, without recourse to overt violence, so the German officer at Tôtes will not attempt to use force upon his victims but engages instead in a combat of wills. There seems little doubt that he will win, since this victory is prefigured by the capitulation of the Rouennais themselves, whose inaction and selfishness has already been stigmatized. The Prussians, on the other hand, are portrayed as dynamic and united. Any movement they make leads to a result, as the introductory passage of the story clearly shows. The narrator associates the invaders with rapidity and decision, characteristics noticeably lacking in their opponents. The German advance is shown as unified and disciplined: 'une masse noire'; 'flots envahisseurs'; 'les avant-gardes des trois corps, juste au même moment, se joignirent'(p. 51). To convey the impression of an irresistible force carrying all before it, they are associated with natural disasters such as floods or earthquakes.

So the first movement is linear, as the invading forces follow in the steps of the retreating French across Normandy towards Dieppe after the capture of Rouen. In their turn the travellers set off on the same route and will eventually reach their goal, but it is the interruption of their journey which forms the central interest of the story. The reader knows that it is essential for the journey to be completed without delay, and must be concerned when an obstacle appears. The confinement of the passengers within their carriage is an opportunity for the narrator to produce information which invites the reader to look beyond the limits of the space which contains the group. The introduction of their past lives endows the passengers with depth and enables the reader to understand their characters. The narration is no longer a straightforward, linear account of a journey from Rouen to Dieppe; the features which could have made it into a travelogue are rapidly dismissed once the setting is established, and the narrator concentrates on the interaction of the fugitives.

As he reveals the past existence of his subjects, the story begins to move through time past. The examination of the motivations of the different characters brings their history into play. When the passengers begin to speak for themselves during their first conversations in the coach, then the reader sees the emergence of another strand of the composition, for each passenger has his own version of the reasons for his actions. This does not always correspond to the information given by the narrator, so the reader finds himself having to interpret contradictory evidence for himself. So not only do the passengers influence each other, they influence the reader also, and the reader's contribution adds another dimension to the story.

During the travellers' stay at the inn, the narrator brings several interesting areas for speculation to the attention of his audience, though they are not equally discussed. The effect of this is to create a variety of distractions for the reader which overlay the desultory pastimes of the hostages themselves. Just as the travellers step out into the village around the inn in an effort to change their situation, so the author provides new questions for consideration which will ensure the reader's involvement.

One such question is that of the moral justification for war, expressed with great liveliness by the innkeeper's wife, who rejoices in the risqué name of Madame Follenvie. She begins by criticism of the enemy :

> Elle raconta toutes ses impressions à l'arrivée des Prussiens, ce qu'ils faisaient, ce qu'ils disaient, les exécrant d'abord parce qu'ils lui coûtaient de l'argent, et, ensuite, parce qu'elle avait deux fils à l'armée. (p. 68)

By calling into question the speaker's sense of values, the narrator stimulates

36

the reader into a re-evaluation of the material provided. How much of Madame Follenvie's apparent patriotism is founded on her concern for her savings ? However much the reader may agree with the notion that it is a fruitless occupation to train men to kill one another, the point loses its altruism when it is associated with the idea of personal economy: 'Faut-il que le pauvre peuple les nourrisse pour n'apprendre rien qu'à massacrer?'(p. 69) Even when the landlady attracts Cornudet's approval by her attack on kings, the cause of all the misery in her opinion, the republican and the citizeness are not really in agreement.

The self-interest of Carré-Lamadon is clearly indicated when the narrator reports on the industrialist's reaction to the discussion.

> M. Carré-Lamadon réfléchissait profondément. Bien qu'il fût fanatique des illustres capitaines, le bon sens de cette paysanne le faisait songer à l'opulence qu'apporteraient dans un pays tant de bras inoccupés et par conséquent ruineux, tant de forces qu'on entretient improductives, si on les employait aux grands travaux industriels qu'il faudra des siècles pour achever. (pp. 69-70)

M. Carré-Lamadon's concern with wasted manpower puts the argument into another perspective, to which the narrator returns when the travellers take their first walk outside the inn. Whatever the expense of their training, of which Madame Follenvie spoke with such feeling, the Prussian soldiers are engaged in peace-time activities usually carried out by women. The local people no longer feel that the invaders are enemies and can sympathise with them as human beings, sharing the idea that they are all—French and German alike—the victims of their rulers, as the beadle says to the count, 'Voyez-vous, Monsieur, entre pauvres gens, faut bien qu'on s'aide... C'est les grands qui font la guerre'(p.72).

For their different reasons the travellers cannot agree with the abolition of national identity, but the experience of their visit to the village makes them think again; neither the democrat nor the assorted conservatives are reassured by what they have seen. It is here that the narrator refers to their political allegiances, which must be considered in any debate on the war. Only Loiseau does not treat the subject with any seriousness. His own interest always comes first, and the narrator punctuates his description of the travellers' gradual discovery of the discrepancy between principle and reality by reference to Loiseau's tireless pursuit of profit in the wine trade.

The narrator's investigation of each character's attitude towards the war intensifies the focus on patriotism. Boule de Suif's sense of responsibility to her nation is shown early by her reaction to Cornudet's criticism of Napoléon III during the journey, and reinforced by her violent reception of the German officers billeted upon her in Rouen. It will require the catalyst of the nuns' ideas on war to change the prostitute's mind, by introducing an argument not previously entertained. In this way the inaction of the travellers as they wait for the prostitute to save them is disguised by the intensity of the argument at the heart of their dilemma. It reaches its climax in the protest voiced by the older nun: 'Et tandis qu'elles étaient arrêtées en route par les caprices de ce Prussien, un grand nombre de Français pouvaient mourir qu'elles auraient sauvés peut-être!'(p. 82) None of this material is overtly discussed by the narrator. He invites the reader to look at a variety of attitudes, but does not draw a conclusion on his behalf, the object being to provoke rather than to reassure.

Other avenues indicated, if not fully explored by the narrator are the travellers' fear of reprisal if the officer does not get his way, female sympathies with the Prussian officer, Madame Carré-Lamadon's penchant for military men of any nation, the unspoken antipathy between Madame Loiseau and the ladies of leisure, and the information that Boule de Suif is herself a mother, albeit an indifferent one. The effect of this scattering of undeveloped topics is to endow an essentially static situation—being held hostage—with apparently random movement which resembles the unpredictability of life itself. The author imposes upon the linear movement of a journey the multi-dimensional scope of ideas that involve past, present and future, and combine the assorted actors in shifting permutations of alliances and antagonisms.

Once the dilemma is resolved, the story resumes its linear form in the journey, and the conclusion neatly balances the opening, which showed hordes of defeated soldiers coming towards the narrator. In the last passage, the coach moves away from the reader, as the passengers escape to the coast.

NARRATIVE TECHNIQUE :
MAUPASSANT'S SELECTIVE REALISM

There is a great deal to admire in the prose style of *Boule de Suif* , and it is not possible to do justice to the author's skill in a few pages, but some features are indicated here, with a critical commentary on the introductory passage of the story in the following chapter.

The opening paragraphs convey the impression of an invisible observer, all-knowing and all-seeing, who has the power to see whole regiments on the move, as if at a distance, and who yet has the ability to focus on details of dress, as if at close range. At the same time, this observer has a memory of the past and an understanding of why things were done. It seems as if he were everywhere and knew everything, for he also knows about the fears and hopes of the citizens of Rouen and what goes on inside their houses. Yet he is not impersonal, for he associates himself with the generality of people in his remarks about the nature of warfare and questions of religious faith—'toute la confiance qu'on nous enseigne' (p. 52)—which may also justify our thinking that the narrator is a Frenchman. If this seems too obvious to mention, then the reader is already the author's willing accomplice.

At other times the narrator is more individual still, for he expresses his own opinion upon the situations and characters that he describes for us in such a way that our opinion of them will be coloured by his. When, for example, he tells us that the merchant-warriors claimed they alone were defending France, he undercuts this ringing pronouncement by adding 'sur leurs épaules de fanfarons.' It is clear that it is the narrator's opinion, and his highly developed sense of irony comes to be shared by the reader, who cannot reject the narrator's assessment of people and situations without finding himself to be in the camp of those selfish and narrow-minded bourgeois who are the targets of criticism.

So the reader is drawn into complicity with the narrator, whose assertions dictate a particular response. The use of capital letters endows the statement 'Car la haine de l'Etranger arme toujours quelques Intrépides prêts à mourir pour une Idée'(p. 53) with sententiousness. Other generalisations serve as a kind of shorthand, where he assumes a readerly concurrence of opinion on such matters as whether prostitutes can speak with fervour: 'avec *cette* chaleur de parole qu'ont parfois les filles pour exprimer leurs emportements naturels'; or whether ladies in high society are ever at a loss what to say in any situation: 'la comtesse surtout montra *cette* condescendance aimable des très nobles dames qu'aucun contact ne peut salir'(p. 63: my emphasis).

More usually, Maupassant tells his story through the actions of the travellers, but here again the apparently impersonal third-person style has various forms, as if the camera-like narrator had a set of lenses to change his focus. There are, for example, the different uses of the third person plural and the singular 'on'. He calls the party 'ils' when they are presented at a distance, physical or moral; in the inn courtyard, when they are about to set out on their journey, and strangers still, we read: 'Ils étaient encore pleins de sommeil'; 'ils causèrent'; 'ils demeuraient immobiles'; 'Ils n'y avaient pas songé'; 'ils se précipitèrent'. In closer focus, where the travellers may be seen as individuals with personal thoughts, however indistinguishable one from another, they become 'on', and we can see this usage combined with the use of 'ils' in the same section where we can also read 'où l'on devait monter en voiture'; 'On se voyait mal'; and 'l'on n'entendait plus'.

Once the travellers have names and identities, however, the sources of information for the reader are multiplied, as each character is a potential mouthpiece, either in reported or direct speech, or the version given by the narrator. In this way, conflicts can be convincingly represented, opposing arguments can be expressed, and secrets brought to light in private conversations. Since direct speech gives an impression of immediacy, Maupassant uses it for the highlights of his tale, sometimes producing pieces of dialogue wholesale without further comment and leaving the reader to assess their value, as when the count questions the coachman in the village café.

In the following dialogue between Boule de Suif and M. Follenvie, however, the interpolations between the spoken words, like stage directions, serve to increase our understanding, so that the reader knows how to interpret the speech.

Il demanda:
'Mademoiselle Elisabeth Rousset?
Boule de Suif tressaillit, se retourna:
'C'est moi.
—Mademoiselle, l'officier prussien veut vous parler
immédiatement.
—A moi?
—Oui, si vous êtes bien mademoiselle Elisabeth Rousset.'
Elle se troubla, réfléchit une seconde, puis déclara carrément:
'C'est possible, mais je n'irai pas.' (p. 67)

In fact, it very much resembles a play, in that some of the "stage instructions" concern the moves the actor should make, while others indicate the emotional state to be conveyed: the narrator becomes producer.

Maupassant takes this dramatic effect further by including episodes that have no sound at all, and rely solely on gesture and movement for their effect, such as the scene in the coach where Boule de Suif, giving way to hunger, is tempted to take out her basket of food, but refrains from doing so because the others have nothing. The drama that follows is enacted in silence, Boule de Suif nibbling delicately at her chicken wing and bread roll, the rest staring and salivating in anguish.

Another feature of the narrative which gives it such liveliness, is the inclusion of figures who make solo speeches, having no material part to play in the action but contributing to the general information which the author wishes the reader to take into consideration. There are four notable "set-piece" speeches in *Boule de Suif*, which help to round out the background of the story. One is Boule de Suif's own outburst against the democratic politics of Cornudet, when he criticises Napoléon III; her political views do not substantially affect the story, but they give depth to her character. Moreover, since the outburst is surprising, it creates a diversion in the train of events. The characters presented by the author seem too energetic to be confined within the bounds of the story concerning them. In attempting to create a sense of realism, the author allows the characters to behave and speak in a lifelike manner. All four of these monologues are punctuated by the speaker's own exclamations and questions, the other three being similarly provocative: Madame Follenvie's speech against war, the village beadle's comments on the army of occupation, which are so astonishing to the count, and Madame

41

Loiseau's impatient tirade against the prostitute. When we consider the episodes of dramatic material built into the story, it is not surprising to learn that since the author's death it has been turned into a play, and later into a film.

There is one last observation to make here on the narrative techniques used by Maupassant: that the effect of naturalness owes much to the way in which the reader accompanies the narrator, constantly at his side, moving within the city of Rouen, joining the travellers in the inn courtyard, and invisibly getting into the carriage with them, so that the journey is seen from inside the vehicle when the travellers are ensconced in it, or from outside when they get out to look for food or help. Inside the inn at Tôtes the narrator discreetly stays downstairs, and the visitors move away from him and the reader. He sees the Loiseau couple in their bedroom, and describes the keyhole gazing that then occurs, but does not himself indulge in such unpleasant behaviour. Similarly, he is present at the interview with the officer in his room upstairs, but only arrives with the party, and leaves with them as they politely bow themselves out.

In other words, the narrator deals only with those matters that are germane to his story. We do not know the life story of the German officer prior to his command at Tôtes, or learn of his feelings each time he is rejected by Boule de Suif; what does Monsieur Follenvie think of the events going on under his roof, and what is his attitude towards the orders he receives ? Each of the characters conceals a certain personal mystery, hinted at by the author, but not explored.

The effect of this technique is twofold. The limitation imposed by the structure of a short story obliges the author to be economical in his composition. By his use of suggestion Maupassant is able to give depth and variety to his work. At the same time, the lack of development or explanation involves the reader in the material, for it is left to him or her to contemplate these enigmas and satisfactorily to resolve them. So it is that the author's own aim, to find 'la vérité choisie et expressive', is realised.

Chapter Four

Critical Commentary

I

Pendant plusieurs jours de suite des lambeaux d'armée en déroute avaient traversé la ville. Ce n'était point de la troupe, mais des hordes débandées. Les hommes avaient la barbe longue et sale, des uniformes en guenilles, et ils avançaient d'une allure molle, sans drapeau, sans régiment. Tous semblaient accablés, éreintés, incapables d'une pensée ou d'une résolution, marchant seulement par habitude, et tombant de fatigue sitôt qu'ils s'arrêtaient. On voyait surtout des mobilisés, gens pacifiques, rentiers tranquilles, pliant sous le poids du fusil; des petits moblots alertes, faciles à l'épouvante et prompts à l'enthousiasme, prêts à l'attaque comme à la fuite; puis, au milieu d'eux, quelques culottes rouges, débris d'une division moulue dans une grande bataille; des artilleurs sombres alignés avec ces fantassins divers; et parfois, le casque brillant d'un dragon au pied pesant qui suivait avec peine la marche plus légère des lignards.

Des légions de franc-tireurs aux appellations héroïques : 'les Vengeurs de la Défaite—les Citoyens de la Tombe—les Partageurs de la Mort'—passaient à leur tour, avec des airs de bandits.

Leurs chefs, anciens commerçants en draps ou en graines, ex-marchands de suif ou de savon, guerriers de circonstance, nommés officiers pour leurs écus ou la longueur de leurs moustaches, couverts d'armes, de flanelle et de galons, parlaient d'une voix retentissante, discutaient plans de campagne, et prétendaient soutenir seuls la France agonisante sur leurs épaules de fanfarons; mais ils redoutaient parfois leurs propres soldats, gens de sac et de corde, souvent braves à outrance, pillards et débauchés.

Les Prussiens allaient entrer dans Rouen, disait-on. (pp. 50-1)

The opening paragraphs of a story must be carefully designed to hold the reader's attention. Here the author establishes contact with the reader with a skill of composition which will be analysed in depth. The title of the story itself can mean nothing in the early stages. Its significance as a half-affectionate, half-pejorative nickname is not revealed until the character is introduced. It is obscure, deliberately so perhaps, in order to catch the reader's imagination.

The reader must therefore hold the title in reserve and consider the description of a defeated army in flight. The subject is introduced and then developed. There is an element of repetition in the first four sentences. Each refers to the same subject, differently expressed, 'des lambeaux d'armée', 'des hordes débandées', 'les hommes' and 'tous'. The first two convey the idea of troops in disorder, the third identifies a section of the whole, and the fourth unites them in a global statement. There is also movement in the verbs 'traverser', 'avancer' and 'marcher'. At each new statement, however, something is added to the narration, giving the effect of closer scrutiny by an observer who has watched the events over a number of days—'Pendant plusieurs jours de suite.' The more the men go by, the less they resemble an army and the more they become individuals. This insight reflects not only their disorderly retreat but also the observer's understanding, for he sees the misery of their condition.

He makes the point that they are no longer united: 'Ce n'était point de la troupe.' The symbol of their cause is no longer there, and the absence of their banner exemplifies the losses they have suffered, physically and morally. There is a sequence of negative expressions in 'ne ... point', 'sans' and 'incapables', reinforcing the idea of loss. All the details betray their lack of morale due to total defeat; 'la barbe longue et sale' and 'des uniformes en guenilles' convey more than simple lack of pride in appearance but suggest rather the endurance of harsh conditions over a period of time. The anaphoric negative expressions 'sans drapeau, sans régiment' also indicate the confusion after a battle and the disorder in which the retreat has taken place. The lack of energy expressed by 'd'une allure molle' is reinforced in the next sentence by the repetition of adjectives expressing physical weariness and mental exhaustion. In fact, the narrator has seen so many fugitives going through the town that he generalises, referring to them as 'tous'. They are no longer a fighting force; their training for aggression is reduced to a reflex action of marching 'par habitude' until they collapse.

The first impression created by the narrator is therefore that of an involved witness who returns each day to watch the passage of a defeated and disorganised mass of men. His observations show him that the men are in no condition to rally and fight again, and that the disaster is final. At the same time, he invites sympathy for their predicament, noticing details that reveal their ordeal and his concern for them.

The second half of the paragraph, although contained in one long sentence, also has four sections, and the more detailed observation expressed in these suggests that the narrator has found an opportunity to draw closer to his subjects. He is able to pick out different uniforms. If in the first half of the paragraph the emphasis is upon the fleeing men, the second half centres on the narrator himself who now expresses some of his personal opinions.

Referring to himself impersonally as 'on', the narrator continues his description prefaced by the verb 'voir'. The vision is more impressionistic than strictly representational, making way for the narrator's thoughts, which are prompted by his glancing observations. He sees 'surtout des mobilisés [...] pliant sous le poids du fusil', but this detail, which indicates their unfitness as fighting men, causes him to extend his reflection into an area which he cannot literally see, but which experience tells him is the case: that their comfortable lives have not prepared them to be soldiers, either physically or psychologically. These men are peace-loving, inclined to a complacency conveyed by the use of 'tranquilles' and connoted by 'rentiers': not only of private means, but accustomed to a life of ease and leisure. After the reservists, the equally unmilitary members of the Garde Mobile are observed, and again the narrator's memory supplies him with the information that they are unreliable as a fighting force. Their dangerous unpredictability is accentuated by adjectives conveying the idea of haste, 'alertes', 'faciles', 'prompts' and 'prêts', the last three concise and expressive in their parallel construction of preposition plus noun. These are arranged in balanced structures of opposing ideas : 'épouvante' is set against 'enthousiasme', and 'attaque' against 'fuite', suggestive of the volatility of these well-meaning but inexperienced young men. Developing the idea of the narrator casting his eyes over the crowds, the author makes him—'puis, au milieu d'eux...'—look into their midst. Details are picked out as the men pass by and items briefly mentioned, as if there were no time to dwell upon anything other than the most obvious features. The narrator's roving eye is caught by colours: 'quelques culottes rouges', 'des artilleurs sombres' and 'le casque brillant d'un dragon'. The lesser numbers of these men leads him to conclude that there has been a great battle and that these are the 'débris', an emotive word which implies large-scale destruction. Again the narrator's assessment of the situation invites the reader's sympathy for the fate of those who did not survive the brutal struggle announced in the choice of the verb 'moudre' for the carnage of the battlefield. The final image is especially poignant as it stresses the sense of loss and humiliation in the weary tread of the cavalryman, a lone survivor isolated amid so many infantry.

However diverse the components of the hordes passing through the city, the overall picture is one of concerted movement. From 'traverser' to 'suivre', the reader sees the retreat, at first in a general and distant way, but finally at closer quarters as the narrator gives his interpretation of events. The canvas showing retreat on an epic scale is given drama by the arrival—and departure—of the guerrilla fighters. Their assorted titles proclaim brotherhood in defiance of the enemy and death suggestive of the spirit of the Revolution of 1789, 'Partageurs', in particular, suggesting socialism. The narrator succeeds in conveying this mixture of bravado and desperation in a kind of shorthand, using the list of their titles to tell their own story of defeat and death. Even as they move out of sight, the narrator adds a comment which suggests his own scepticism: 'Avec des airs de bandits' seems to refer rather more to their mutinous appearance than to their real aggression.

The narrator is apparently standing still while everyone else moves around him. The waves of soldiers and stragglers have gone 'à leur tour', to be replaced by their officers. The eye of the narrator takes in their appearance, characterised by a combination of ostentatiously warlike trappings and warm clothing. The order in which he lists these features, 'couverts d'armes, de flanelle et de galons', reduces their wearers' military competence to the level of concern for their own safety, which makes his judgement of them immediately manifest. Other remarks show that he has some prior knowledge of the men of whom he speaks, for he refers to their former occupations. The burden of his information is that they are unsuited to be in charge of men's lives, a statement so important that it is made four times. The effect is to belittle the title of 'chefs' by associating it with the words 'anciens commerçants', 'ex-marchands', 'guerriers de circonstance', 'nommés officiers pour leurs écus', all of which assure the reader that these men can only play at being soldiers. The reference to trade is linked to the idea of wealth amassed by dealing in necessary but unglamorous commodities. Is there also a hint that anyone who is able to make a fortune out of such things cannot be honest ? The idea of pretence is heavily underlined by the ironic 'pour leurs écus ou la longueur de leurs moustaches', reinforced by the use of 'couverts' to suggest not only the sense of being protected by an abundance of weapons and costume, but also the sense of hiding beneath them, as in a disguise.

When the narrator has prepared his introduction he tells the reader—for the first time—what there is to hear as well as to see, in his use of the verbs 'parler', 'discuter' and 'prétendre'. The narration is not purely objective reporting however, for the narrator passes on his own opinion that the speakers are 'fanfarons', which reduces the stature of their plans of campaign. The narrator's derogatory opinion is emphasized by his observation that the officers are afraid of their own men, while the soldiers are given the attributes of savagery and wild daring usually reserved for an enemy, 'gens de sac et de corde', 'braves à outrance, pillards et débauchés.'

Up to this point in the introduction to the story, the author controls three different levels of narration. The first is related directly to the experience of the observer who recounts the movement of troops in flight through a city, gradually confiding his thoughts on the nature of what he sees until the point at which he begins to reveal his personal knowledge of them. This is connected with a second level of interpretation where questions arise as a result of what the narrator has to tell, such as the fact that this is an army on the run, that a great disaster has occurred and that it might have been avoided. The third level makes direct contact with the reader, who is thus drawn into the narrator's story, passing through stages of curiosity and sympathy, drawn closer to the action by the supposition that he can share in what the observer sees and hears. Yet he is still held in subjection by the narrator's omission of more precise information which might permit the reader to form his own opinion of the events described. Indeed, the reader may know of them already and might prefer his own assessment of the drama enacted.

Perhaps the author has his own reasons for choosing to keep the reader in suspense from the beginning. The subject of the collection of stories *Les Soirées de Médan* which included *Boule de Suif* was known to be the Franco-Prussian war of 1870-71, so the reader of 1880, remembering the events of ten years ago, could be looking for some clue to enable him to place his recollections more exactly. Before he is able to do this, the author endeavours to make sure that the reader's mind is correctly attuned to the points he wants to make. The reader must understand the distress caused by loss of morale; he must see again the reality of defeat, when the trained fighting force is decimated and has to be replaced by inexperienced and untrained men who cannot hope to fill the places of their predecessors and turn disaster into victory; he has to accept that the blame for defeat lies with those whom society most respects—the financially successful. Only then can the author allow his narrator to pronounce words capable of interpretation by the reader's own experience.

'La France agonisante' can only be a reference to that period of the war which followed upon the great defeat of Sedan in September 1870 , when France's fortunes took a definitive turn for the worse, and the single sentence

Les Prussiens allaient entrer dans Rouen, disait-on.

enables the reader to situate the story much more precisely. However, it is not so much for its historical content that the sentence standing alone is so effective, but for its emotive impact. That the traditional enemies of France should be about to enter one of its great cities, formerly a bastion of independence and moreover, not in the front line of French cities near the German border, is deeply distressing. The information signifies a disaster of great magnitude. The unthinkable has happened.

The importance of this sentence as a watershed for the story is emphasized by the author's use of reported speech for this information, a departure from the third-person description of the earlier sequence, which will be resumed in the ensuing narration. It also marks a subtle change in the stance and focus of the narrator himself. From this point onwards, he acquires a new status as a man who knows Normandy and is familiar with the city of Rouen and its inhabitants past and present. He is well-informed on a wide range of subjects, from the background of individual citizens to the progress of the Franco-Prussian War. Certain features of his character, already apparent in the introduction, such as his eye for significant detail and his ironic humour, will be given more expression as his detached and disparaging attitude towards his fellow men and women colours the description of events.

It is customary, when discussing the work of Maupassant, to use terms such as "realist" and "realism", and in the literal sense this may be applicable here. The author is presenting something that really did happen. The events he portrays in the exposition to his story actually took place. They have been documented by other reporters who had no intention of entertaining the public by their recording of the capture of a city. The effect of documentation in the story is certainly enhanced by the author's choice of a knowledgeable storyteller whose credibility is supported by reference to undisputed facts of which he seems to have been an eye-witness. However, Maupassant himself knew that careful selection of information could be more effective than wholesale repetition, and explained the importance of the uniquely expressive detail in the preface to his novel *Pierre et Jean* . Such a formula does not however explain his use of irony, which has such an influence on the mind of the reader. The author's determination to ensure that the reader shares his point of view is clearly exhibited in the second part of the exposition.

II

La Garde nationale qui, depuis deux mois, faisait des reconnaissances très prudentes dans les bois voisins, fusillant parfois ses propres sentinelles, et se préparant au combat quand un petit lapin remuait sous des broussailles, était rentrée dans ses foyers. Ses armes, ses uniformes, tout son attirail meurtrier, dont elle épouvantait naguère les bornes des routes nationales à trois lieues à la ronde, avaient subitement disparu.

Les derniers soldats français venaient enfin de traverser la Seine pour gagner Pont-Audemer par Saint-Sever et Bourg-Achard; et, marchant après tous, le général, désespéré, ne pouvant rien tenter avec ces loques disparates, éperdu lui-même dans la grande débâcle d'un peuple habitué à vaincre et désastreusement battu malgré sa bravoure légendaire, s'en allait à pied entre deux officiers d'ordonnance.

Puis un calme profond, une attente épouvantée et silencieuse avaient plané sur la cité. Beaucoup de bourgeois bedonnants, émasculés par le commerce, attendaient anxieusement les vainqueurs, tremblant qu'on ne considérât comme une arme leurs broches à rôtir ou leurs grands couteaux de cuisine.

La vie semblait arrêtée; les boutiques étaient closes, la rue muette. Quelquefois un habitant, intimidé par ce silence, filait rapidement le long des murs.

L'angoisse de l'attente faisait désirer la venue de l'ennemi.

(p. 51)

Since the narrator's credibility has been established by the foregoing part of his tale, what he has to say next must benefit from the confidence that the reader already has in his opinions. This is a very useful device, because his words might not otherwise meet with approval. Another factor brought into play here is the reference to the past. This again gives plausibility to the narration, with reference to the activities of the Garde nationale and the real place names cited on the route of the army's retreat. The description of the Garde nationale is composed of statements: 'La Garde nationale [...] faisait des reconnaissances'; 'fusillant parfois'; 'se préparant au combat.' These would be quite proper activities for them. It is the additions made by the narrator which give bias to the statements, turning these examples of military preparation into accusations of incompetence. The tardiness of this preparation is hinted at by the remark 'depuis deux mois', since the war had already been going badly before that time, but the other qualifications emphasize the fearfulness of the men supposed to be protecting their homeland. Like the rabbits whose movements give them such cause for alarm, the guard stay cautiously in their local woods, act impulsively and dart down their burrows at the least sign of trouble: 'était rentrée dans ses foyers' and 'avaient subitement disparu.' In other words, they do exactly the opposite of what is expected of them, because they are not inspired by the courage of patriotism. The comic effect of the image of men behaving like rabbits is developed in the evocation of their martial display of weapons and uniform. The 'attirail meurtrier' loses its effect when the narrator adds that what it 'épouvantait naguère' was only the kilometre markers bordering the highways along which they beat a retreat.

But in case the reader should fear that these are the words of an idle spectator who is happy to stand by and mock others' deficiencies, the author makes the narrator express his respect for the army in defeat. The irony is replaced by sympathy as the narrator paints a picture of the last soldiers crossing the Seine, as if he had been there himself to see the order in which things were done and to have observed the honourable detail that the general went last. The effect of the narration is heightened by the inclusion of such emotive words as 'désespéré', 'éperdu' and 'désastreusement'. The pessimism of 'ne pouvant rien tenter avec ces loques disparates' and 'la grande débâcle' is complemented by the words 'un peuple habitué à vaincre' and 'sa bravoure légendaire', although it is obvious that, in the circumstances, faith in past bravery was not enough to save France. So the writer is able to convey a variety of feelings in this short passage encompassing the expectation of victory and the humiliation of defeat, an idea poignantly expressed in the final image of the army's leader following his men on foot.

The first half of the exposition and the second are linked by the idea of continuous movement. Once again the principal verbs are those of movement, 'rentrer', 'disparaître', 'traverser','marcher', 's'en aller'. With the departure of the troops hope fades, and the narrator looks inwards, both literally, into the houses of the citizens of Rouen, and figuratively, into their minds. Movement ceases as the period of waiting for the enemy begins.

The narrator sees the act of waiting as a kind of fate hanging over the city. It is motionless, silent and full of fear, and these three qualities are evoked throughout this section: 'un calme profond, une attente épouvantée et silencieuse.' The people are afraid, waiting anxiously as one might expect, but the narrator complicates this natural emotion by reintroducing the subject of the cowardice of his compatriots, as in the description of the officers. Again there are prosperous citizens unsuited to the immediate task of defending their city. The censorious narrator depicts them as unmanly and unfit. Their chosen pursuit of trade is to blame for their moral as well as their physical weakness, for it has warped their minds, making them cautious and calculating. Their greed has swelled their stomachs, a theme repeated in the reference to their roasting-spits and kitchen knives. They are already defeated by their cowardliness; for them the enemy are already 'les vainqueurs', and they tremble in fear of unwittingly provoking them.

It is indeed a kind of death, especially in a commercial centre where closed shops and silent streets mean no profits. The narrator has seen and heard it all for himself. Ever watchful, he recalls the detail which will make it memorable for the reader, as the image of a terrified citizen rushing for safety through the silent streets unites the themes of stillness, 'la vie semblait arrêtée, les boutiques étaient closes', silence and fear, 'la rue muette'; 'intimidé par ce silence', while the expression 'filait rapidement le long des murs' reinforces the sense of menace and dread.

In these few lines, Maupassant has outlined the reasons for the defeat not only of Normandy, but of France. He has accused the administration of incompetence, and with some carefully chosen examples indicates how those who could best have come to the help of their country considered only their own interests and effectively betrayed the armies of France to the invaders. The hypocrisy of the bourgeoisie has however insulated them from any self-criticism, and the acts of collaboration with the enemy which will inevitably follow are announced in the grim but plausible concluding statement which precedes the eye-witness description of the arrival of the Prussians in Rouen.

The result of the introductory passage is to attract the reader's sympathy for those who have shown patriotism in their efforts to defend France and to identify for him at the same time those selfish natives of France whose conduct deserves blame. The message is clear: the hypocritical bourgeoisie of France was as much responsible for the defeat in the war of 1870-71 as the invaders from beyond the Rhine.

Chapter Five

Characterisation

(1) APPEARANCE

In Gustave Flaubert's warm praise of the drawing of the characters in *Boule de Suif* —'Le paysage et les personnages se voient'—is indicated the very quality that makes them so distinctive, for the author constructs his characters in such a way that they have a visual quality, although this is not strictly representational. Unlike his predecessor Balzac, for example, Maupassant does not refer, in a physical description, to any detail that could not be seen by the narrator / spectator in his current circumstances. Indeed occasionally one might accuse the author of inflicting the narrator with "tunnel vision", so intently is his gaze focused upon his subjects. One has the impression that he is peering at them, measuring them like a painter preparing a portrait, sometimes full length, sometimes head and shoulders, sometimes the face only, although others, Madame Follenvie for example, whose one long speech is of such importance for the theme of the story, are given no distinguishing characteristics at all. She is presented only as a voice to the reader, although she is a physical presence for the travellers.

The extent of Maupassant's human descriptions is interestingly revealed in illustrated editions of his stories. The first collection to include an illustrated *Boule de Suif* , published 1899-1904 by Ollendorff, with drawings by Jeanniot, is well worth consulting for the delightful sketches of certain episodes, especially those of the travellers wedged together in the coach. But they reveal also the partiality with which some persons are described whereas others are hardly endowed with physical features, so that the illustrator, apparently reluctant to invent what is not there in the text, fudges over the less clear appearances.

The Travellers

To the aristocrat, the Count Hubert de Bréville, Maupassant gives an appearance which is already well known to his readers, that of the first Bourbon king of France, Henri IV. Maupassant reproduces the archaic spelling of the word 'roy', perhaps to underline the count's deliberate attempt to recreate a historical appearance which would be flattering to himself. He therefore does not need to describe the neat beard, the upturned moustaches, the alert glance or the slightly cynical expression, for they are all familiar. The narrator is free instead to make the point that this resemblance is important to the bearer of it, who 's'efforçait d'accentuer, par les artifices de sa toilette, sa ressemblance naturelle'(p. 57). The fact that the Bréville family owed its distinctive features to this monarch's seduction of an ancestress is glossed over. No-one now would care to remind the count of this fact; only the narrator's ironic 'suivant une légende glorieuse pour la famille' highlights its interest as an indication of the count's vanity and pride in his title. The countess does not share her husband's noble descent and it seems unlikely that they would have moved in the same social circles. The daughter of 'un petit armateur de Nantes'(p. 57) is portrayed as an unlikely bride for the count—though the reasons are unfathomable to local gossip—, hence the emphasis on the importance of respectability. Her exclusive receptions win the admiration and flatter the vanity of her peers, while her acquired rank establishes a barrier to the curiosity of the lower orders. Her success in society may suggest an irresistible alliance of beauty with ambition, but the narrator cites no physical attributes that would confirm this. In fact, his mockery of this aristocratic *mésalliance* is partly aimed at those scruples that cede before the prestige of her royal lover.

Similarly, only the husband in the Loiseau couple has an outer shell; it is of a caricatural nature—'de taille exiguë, il présentait un ventre en ballon surmonté d'une face rougeaude entre deux favoris grisonnants'(p. 56), with a comic shape and a sketch of a face. His wife is 'grande' and 'forte' but there the description of her appearance ends. Loiseau's 'activité joyeuse' is limited in the coach to his roving eyes, but the development of the story shows him trotting busily out to get orders for his wine, and on the last night at the inn wishing they could dance, with characteristic animation.

Of the Carré-Lamadon couple, only the wife is described physically, but without detail. She is 'beaucoup plus jeune que son mari', 'toute petite, toute mignonne, toute jolie, pelotonnée dans ses fourrures.' Her husband's dignity is evident to his companions, but no single item of his outward appearance is provided.

Since it is possible to take for granted the costume of nuns, unless one is knowledgeable enough to distinguish between the different orders (which the narrator does not choose to do), the two sisters travelling in the party are at once distinctive and anonymous. Although their faces are differentiated they are in all other ways indistinguishable, acting in concert. Apparently the discipline of their lives has taken away their individuality.

The two remaining travellers receive more, but very different attention. Cornudet's past is recounted as an indication of the quality of the man. Of his appearance, his fingers, teeth and beard, are mentioned, and 'sa barbe rousse' will feature regularly throughout the story, as Cornudet alternately strokes or twists his fingers in it, according to whether his mind is at ease or in turmoil, a sort of emotional barometer. On stepping down from the coach at the request of the officer, 'le démoc tourmentait d'une main tragique et un peu tremblante sa longue barbe roussâtre'(p. 66); as he drinks beer at the inn, 'sa grande barbe, qui avait gardé la nuance de son breuvage aimé, semblait tressaillir de tendresse'(p. 68); he sits by the fire smoking his pipe, at which point we learn that the use of tobacco has stained his teeth, and again there is a reference to his restless fingers, 'il passait d'un air satisfait ses longs doigts maigres dans ses longs cheveux gras'(p. 73); when the other travellers celebrate Boule de Suif's downfall, Cornudet's disgust is shown by his pulling at his beard 'qu'il semblait vouloir allonger encore'(pp. 84-5); and at the end, when all except Boule de Suif eat their provisions, Cornudet's beard is starred with crumbs of boiled egg yolk.

If Cornudet's physique is reduced to a beard, Boule de Suif's appearance is translated into a portrait reminiscent of those curious allegorical paintings where the profile is composed of assorted objects related to the character, (such as an allegory of summer with features composed of a veritable harvest festival of fruit and vegetables). The mere fact of the prostitute's nickname is of course sufficient to indicate her appearance, and the features that the author chooses to enhance, her fingers, bust, and face are carefully associated with the idea of food and feeding, in a way that is doubly significant, both for the depiction of the prostitute's self-indulgence in matters of appetite, and for the implications of her profession, where her body is offered as a consumer product. Her round figure is 'grasse à lard' and her swollen fingers are 'pareils à des chapelets de courtes saucisses.' 'Ronde de partout', she has 'une gorge énorme qui saillait sous sa robe.' The fatness which seems about to burst out of its casing—the image of her fingers as sausages is continued in the reference to her skin "luisante et tendue"—is rendered agreable by the reference to 'sa fraîcheur'. The subsequent evocation of apples and peonies combines the ideas of ripeness and gratification. The flower-bud is about to blossom, and the same promise is suggested in the half-closed eyes and moist mouth of Boule de Suif herself. Rumour has it that she is 'pleine de qualités innappréciables', and presumably able to fulfil the promise she offers.

Maupassant had intended to make more specific reference to her distended stomach and lack of waistline, but on Flaubert's recommendation, he left out these grosser details. Her face is described in such a way as to sound almost botanical rather than human, in spite of its attractiveness, with the references to apples and peonies delineated prosaically as 'là dedans', 'en haut', and 'en bas'. This creates the impression, as it was no doubt meant to, of an objective portrayal given by a detached observer, who isolates the most striking features of an appearance and communicates them as exactly as possible to the reader. Nevertheless, it is interesting to note that the prostitute is the only one of the characters whose eyes are recorded. Her look is allowed to speak for her, as if she were the only one for whom the narrator has some feeling, looking directly into her face. This channel of communication, so unusual in the story, suggests a bond between Boule de Suif and the narrator which in turn promotes a sense of empathy in the reader. Of course, some of her features also convey a touch of colour, making the portrait more vivid. In fact, were it not for Loiseau's rosy face, the red-gold beard of Cornudet and

Boule de Suif's apple cheeks, the entire party would be in monochrome.

From this brief review of the appearance of the travellers, it is clear that we must look further for their characterisation, since their reflection in the eye of the narrator is partial, in both senses of the word. Their unequal value in the telling of the story, coupled with their more dynamic existence as moral forces, sets a limited value on their appearance, which is discarded as soon as they have been situated in their context. In this respect, Maupassant has greater affinity with the classical authors of the Ancien Régime than with innovators of his own time.

We should bear in mind that the author may have chosen to omit certain details of his characters' physical appearance because he did not wish them to be identifiable. If Carré-Lamadon is modelled on Pouyer-Quertier, then perhaps it was better not to be too specific. A detailed portrayal of Adrienne Legay as Boule de Suif, or Charles Cord'homme as Cornudet would affect only a limited audience and serve no purpose. Only significant detail is retailed by the narrator, thus giving the reader the impression that he is sharing a true experience. One of the "appearances", however, is no more than an outer shell, and remains otherwise invisible, existing by virtue of his uniform alone.

The Prussian Officer

So perfunctory is Maupassant's portrayal of the Prussian officer, that most of the character's "lines" are spoken, not by the man himself but by the landlord—note the use of the factitive construction 'fait demander' (pp. 75, 81). The trappings of his appearance, rather than the man himself, play a part even before the travellers have their first sight of him. He is a series of sounds which the passengers can already interpret, the noise of his sabre scabbard dragging on the ground, hence a cavalryman, and a voice speaking German, a detail so terrifying in itself that they fear to get out of their coach.

His first appearance is certainly centre stage, 'en pleine lumière', but the picture of him is surely not truly such as to inspire terror in the beholder. His concern with his looks and consequence seem to dominate every scene involving this young man who has no name and who is quite isolated from the rest of humanity. For he is seen to talk with no-one during the whole episode, except in the interview with the travellers, which is quite devoid of personal warmth. His height, which might be a feature of domineering strength, is weakened by the qualification that he is 'excessivement mince et blond.' Not even his Teutonic blondness is allowed to be an attraction, as the theme of thinness is renewed in his straight-haired moustache, 's'amincissant indéfiniment', and of excessive length, like a straggling plant, 'terminée par un seul fil blond si mince.' This is no Nordic warrior, more a dancing partner of suspiciously slim figure and nipped-in waist. Any humanity, any point of contact with the outside world, is cancelled by the lack of reference to eyes or sight in this face; there is nothing to redeem the 'pli tombant' of his mouth or the chilling effect of his stilted French.

There is moreover a deliberately comic effect in the demeaning reference to his uniform cap, a style not worn in the French army. His military headgear loses its effect, since it resembles (as the narrator points out) a livery of a more domestic kind. Comic also is the laboured inspection of the travellers' passes, at the end of which 'il disparut'. His abrupt disappearance when duty no longer requires his presence underlines the distance between himself and the fugitives. They have nothing to say to him, and his departure is marked by a sense of relief as they draw breath once more.

At the brief meeting in his room, the officer is posed as for a painting, lounging in a way expressive of total unconcern for the niceties of etiquette or his visitors' feelings. The narrator underlines the lack of movement, for the officer is 'étendu dans un fauteuil, les pieds sur la cheminée, fumant une longue pipe de porcelaine, et enveloppé par une robe de chambre flamboyante, dérobée sans doute à quelque bourgeois de mauvais goût'(p. 74) and, failing to make any of the movements expected when the visitors enter, 'ne se leva pas, ne les salua pas, ne les regarda pas.' The stolen dressing gown is added proof that the officer's taste is not shared by the more discriminating narrator, who finds it 'de mauvais goût'. The fact that it was part of the officer's spoils of war is a further indictment of his character

59

and this criticism is soundly reinforced when the narrator summarises him as 'un magnifique échantillon de la goujaterie naturelle au militaire victorieux.'

Unacceptable as he becomes after his proposition to Boule de Suif, the officer produces a not unfavourable effect upon the ladies when they are out walking that is ironically opposite to the narrative comments; they are impressed by the same slimness and military bearing which the narrator ridicules by the scornful 'taille de guêpe' and 'les genoux écartés'(p. 77). Again his appearance is important. The rest of the sequence is dumb show, as he communicates his respect for the ladies and disdain for the men by movement only. The narrator's precise observation about the military way of walking has the effect of diminishing the individual, who becomes a caricature. He does not appear again. Apparently an instrument of Fate, the officer's personality has no other role to play in the drama. He is seen as a strutting uniform or a languid dressing-gown, and it is from this scarecrow that the defeated French must fly.

Writing some seven years later, in the 'Etude sur le Roman' which is usually published as the preface to *Pierre et Jean* (1887), Maupassant argues that the realist novelist, if he wishes to show reality, must avoid 'la photographie banale' of casually perceived data but concentrate instead on 'les détails caractéristiques utiles'. His contention is that life is indiscriminate and unfocused, 'la vie [...] laisse tout au même plan', whereas art has a duty to be selective, in order to produce 'la vérité spéciale'. The conclusion is that "Realists" is not an appropriate title for writers like himself: 'les Réalistes de talent devraient s'appeler plutôt des Illusionistes.' The descriptive element of the characterisation in *Boule de Suif* shows that the writer had already decided to aim for 'la vision plus complète, plus saisissante, plus probante que la réalité même.'

(2) PSYCHOLOGY

By providing the motivation for his characters' actions Maupassant sets out to bring the reader closer to his material, for his idea of making his writing live was to appeal to the reader's own experience, presenting recognisable beings with credible behaviour, and this in turn can only be achieved if the author is true to himself. In the 'Etude sur le Roman', Maupassant's view of the apparent diversity of characters is that in fact they all derive from the same person—the author's own self, or his 'moi' as he calls it in this summary of his argument:

> Nous ne diversifions donc nos personnages qu'en changeant l'âge, le sexe, la situation sociale et toutes les circonstances de la vie de notre moi que la nature a entouré d'une barrière d'organes infranchissable.

In other words, for each character he creates, the author has to ask himself what he would do if he were that character, so in the case of *Boule de Suif* we must imagine Maupassant putting himself inside the head of each character in turn. He argued that however this was done, there still remained the problem of disguising the author from the reader, who must not be able to recognise the common source of all the characters, and this is a task which calls for all the writer's skill. Perhaps here Maupassant does less than justice to the reader, who is going to perform the same action in reverse, by imagining himself to be all the characters in turn, and endowing them with his personal experience, thus perhaps prising them away from the control of their creator. In Maupassant's case, however, the author's grasp of his material is such that the reader shares the author's view of events conveyed by his narrator.

The intending author of a short story such as *Boule de Suif* must necessarily concentrate his material, reducing it to what is most useful for his purposes. Just as the physical descriptions are tailored to requirements, so the motivations of the characters are reduced to apply to immediate circumstances, providing insights into the behaviour of the actors in the story. This is particularly necessary because none of the characters is likely always to tell the truth; there is always something in reserve, not meant for general consumption, but which the reader needs to know if he is to form an opinion and play his proper part in evaluating what he reads.

Maupassant's achievement in this story is his success in creating tension between the characters, who are constantly shifting ground, changing sides and forming alliances without declaring their true interests. He provides each individual with motivations, usually base and selfish, and then sets him in a framework (bourgeois society, religion, patriotism) which obliges him to mask these unacceptable values. Since, however, the baser instincts are stronger than the behaviour assumed for the occasion, each character is a victim of his own hypocrisy. At the same time, the characters cannot successfully ally with each other, although there are occasions when they would like to use each other's strength; hence they are also exposed to exploitation by each other.

The travelling party is composed of people who would not in ordinary circumstances meet, or have any contact with each other. They are essentially incompatible, thrown together by extraordinary events. Because of this they have no common ground, and are shown trying to find some form of equilibrium which will permit them to co-exist in their unusual state. It is obvious that it is social class that has kept them apart, and that the count and countess might know the Carré-Lamadons, but not the Loiseau couple, and certainly not the others. The nuns have chosen to withdraw from that world in which the others move. Polite society has rejected Cornudet, 'la terreur des gens respectables', and the prostitute is a social outcast, 'une honte publique'.

Their sense of social class divides them as their journey begins, but urbanity permits them to "bend" these divisions in order to pass the time in company. Although the Carré-Lamadons belong to 'une caste supérieure' to the Loiseau couple, they all, together with the aristocrats, appear as representatives of the conservative forces in society:

> Ces six personnes formaient le fond de la voiture, le côté de la société rentée, sereine et forte, des honnêtes gens autorisés qui ont de la Religion et des Principes. (p. 57)

The authorial use of capitals is a clear signal of ironic comment on a clichéd group representation of respectability and bourgeois values.

Having an "authorised" tongue, as it were, in common, 'le côté de la société rentée' is able to fraternise. In the assurance of their common interest, money, a count, a textile manufacturer and a wine merchant are united. Their wives are also united by a triple alliance against the prostitute: 'Elles devaient faire comme un faisceau de leurs dignités d'épouses.' Neither of these "fronts" is durable and, under pressure, will not be reasserted until the travellers are able to leave the hotel at Tôtes. The narrator's confidences to the reader show already the differences between them. To mask their socially unacceptable selfishness and concern with material wealth and personal well-being at the expense of others, each has a disguise. In Loiseau, it is his hearty jolliness, his willingness to make jokes and pass the time with cheerful company; nevertheless he is a scoundrel and a thief ready to exploit any situation to his own advantage, and beneath his thin veneer of manners he is entirely without scruple. In Carré-Lamadon, it is his solid worthiness, his respectable standing in society as an employer and a figure in local government. In fact, his status is due to time-serving politics and unscrupulous ambition, which he disguises from himself and others by nostalgic reference to chivalry.

In the count, already referred to as a 'grand seigneur dix fois millionnaire' yet complaining of losses that represent very little for him, the condescending graciousness towards those less fortunate disguises greed. When Boule de Suif humbly offers him food that he has failed to provide for himself, he is able to accept in lordly manner, 'prenant son grand air de gentilhomme.'

The wives are equally two-faced, each having less amiable characteristics that are hidden by their social manner, although the countess shows greater discretion than Madame Loiseau, who cannot resist comment where the former relies on gesture. To the observer an action speaks as loudly as words, and the narrator can equalize observed and recorded responses. This is well demonstrated at the moment when Boule de Suif reappears after her surrender to the enemy: 'Mais la comtesse s'en aperçut et prévint son mari d'un signe. Il haussa les épaules comme pour dire: "Que voulez-vous ? ce n'est pas ma faute." Mme Loiseau eut un rire muet de triomphe, et murmura: "Elle pleure sa honte"'(p. 88).

The democrat Cornudet is separated from them by his opposition to the Empire and the Church, for his political ideas are immediately unacceptable to all the other travellers, and their scornful attitude towards him is at once conveyed in the pejorative way he is tagged, in abbreviated form indicating a caricatural reduction of his views. The one character who might have most understanding for his cause both as a patriot and as one of society's oppressed, is the one who most energetically voices her criticism of him, and thus Boule de Suif, who has forfeited social standing, suddenly finds she has the political sympathy of her critics. Yet it is Cornudet who appears to have done most to contribute to the defence of the city, albeit in a way which is slyly mocked by the narrator. Boule de Suif's patriotic attempt at violence upon the Prussian billeted in her home attracts more consideration than the somewhat ambivalent 'ardeur incomparable'(p. 58) of Cornudet's contribution. He also shows solidarity with the prostitute upon their first meeting with the Prussian officer, as they leave the coach with an attempt at dignity. It would be a mistake, though, to see Cornudet as a patriotic democrat continuing the fight alone, for he too is on the coach with the fleeing bourgeois, and his concern for his creature comforts seems to outweigh other commitments. For him the consumption of beer and tobacco has become synonymous with revolutionary activity. He has passive attributes only, being 'inoffensif et serviable', and his final revenge on his equally spineless compatriots seems a poor exchange for the attack he failed to make on the enemy.

The two nuns, seemingly intent on spiritual salvation only, deliberately isolated from the other travellers either by their absorption in their prayers, or their retreat while in Tôtes to the local priest's house, are paradoxically the most pragmatic of all. They have all the single-mindedness of true parasites, contributing nothing but taking all they can get. The elder nun shows decisiveness and common sense, if called upon. When Madame Carré-Lamadon faints, and her husband panics, it is the elder nun who declares that the cause is merely lack of food and assists by giving the lady a glass of Boule de Suif's wine; until this point she has been content to partake of the prostitute's food herself, eating quickly and without regard to others. The narrator is unwilling to allow religion to occupy the moral high ground, for he suggests that the elder nun's advice to the countess on the subject of sacrifice is ambiguous. Either it is deliberately given, with a pretence of not understanding the intention—'une de ces ententes tacites, de ces complaisances voilées'—, in which case the nun is guilty of treachery towards the prostitute, or else she is stupid and the betrayal is due to 'une secourable bêtise'. In neither case is the prostitute's welfare considered. Once her sacrifice is made, the nuns offer no comfort and express no gratitude; they are aligned once more with the bourgeois members of the party. But on each occasion when they have expressed their idea of the appropriate action to take, they have taken no action to accomplish the recommended deed themselves. They are quite passive. Whether by the gift of food for her travelling companions or by the giving of herself to the Prussian officer, it is Boule de Suif who bears the cost.

As the journey of escape begins, the enemies of the travellers are the weather and the Prussians. As the journey continues, the weather is perhaps not so much an obstacle as enemy occupation, represented in the story by the figure of the officer at Tôtes. Because Boule de Suif is a supplementary obstacle to the continuation of the journey, she becomes in turn the enemy, possibly more detested than the Prussian because the travellers already find her presence disconcerting and a challenge to their complacency. At first their reaction is to express their disdain, but when they have eaten her food, they feel some obligation to talk to her: 'Donc on causa, avec réserve d'abord, puis, comme elle se tenait fort bien, on s'abandonna davantage'(p. 63). Her account of her reason for leaving the city gains their approval, and her political opinions awaken a response in the respectable bourgeois wives whose instincts lead them to admire strong government, so that they are, in spite of themselves, 'attirées vers cette prostituée pleine de dignité, dont les sentiments ressemblaient si fort aux leurs'(p. 65).

They are not so sympathetic when she refuses the officer's request, and the subsequent days see a retreat from the first general outcry—'C'était une clameur de réprobation contre ce soudard ignoble'(p. 75)—when the proposition is made. By the second day they are beginning to turn against her, condemning her resistance by their own impatience to depart, and resenting her independence, although no one dares to admit such demeaning thoughts.

In fact, the married women are secretly attracted by the officer's status and appearance and cherish unavowable dreams of being ravished by him. These immoral longings are doubly inadmissible because they are also unpatriotic. Madame Carré-Lamadon is happy to compare the enemy favourably with French officers she has met in Rouen, and Madame Loiseau notes Madame Carré-Lamadon's secret jealousy when Boule de Suif finally goes to bed with the officer. Nevertheless, the ladies are obliged to maintain a façade of affronted dignity when the officer greets them outside the inn, and it is the narrator who points up the satire in the situation which leads the wives to express their sympathy for the officer's sexual deprivation and to agree that he shows commendable restraint in sparing the married women. The fact that they have been spared is an important factor in their increasing resentment of the prostitute and is expressed in the spitefulness of their conspiracy against her. The refinement of their hypocrisy attracts comment from the narrator for its prurient subtlety:

> Ces dames surtout trouvaient des délicatesses de tournures, des subtilités d'expression charmantes, pour dire les choses les plus scabreuses. Un étranger n'aurait rien compris, tant les précautions du langage étaient observées. (p. 79)

In their turn the men show that Boule de Suif's plight has its funny side for them, and they are able to make jokes about it. No one can escape from the narrator's merciless observation. The count tells 'des plaisanteries un peu risquées', Loiseau indulges in 'des grivoiseries plus raides', and all acknowledge the truth of 'la pensée brutalement exprimée' of Madame Loiseau herself.

As a result of their complicity, communication with Cornudet and Boule de Suif becomes less free, and by the next morning no-one wants to talk to the prostitute. There is significance in the development that shows the party able to talk freely with each other only when she is absent, thus defining the gap that has opened between the travellers. Now they are able at last to say amongst themselves those things that they hardly wished to admit to themselves earlier.

It seems that the presence of the prostitute reinforces the characters' mask of bourgeois respectability. Once she is away, they become what they never thought to be. The women behave as if they were selling flesh in a brothel, under an eventual compulsion deliberately reminiscent of the picnic in the coach, when their initial reluctance to accept help from an inferior gave way to necessity. The men aid and abet in 'cette aventure polissonne', then lay their plans for ensnaring the prostitute as if it were their patriotic duty, and they were carrying out some dangerous mission. The enthusiasm which they bring to accomplishing the downfall of their compatriot contrasts ironically with their faint-heartedness in the defence of their native land. Their sudden "bravery" is deflated by the narrator's mockery in his choice of military vocabulary: 'On prépara longuement le blocus...'(p. 79)

It would be naïve to pretend that the joy of the travellers upon the news of their release derives only from the permission to leave. Their behaviour the following day confirms that the collapse of the prostitute's dignity marks the restoration of their pride, which has been so sorely exposed by hers. However great the Prussian menace to French independence, the respectability of the bourgeois, threatened by the prostitute, has been maintained.

The depths of Maupassant's pessimism are infinite, as later writings reveal. In *Boule de Suif*, the ironic humour which shows all elements of the former imperial society dependent for their salvation upon a prostitute, who is sent to her assignation with the enemy with the blessing of the Church's representatives, is accompanied by a vision of deep disillusionment. No aspect of contemporary life is free from the taint of materialism: church, state, army, marriage, motherhood, patriotism, all disappoint the idealistic views to which the characters themselves pretend. The 'sauveur inconnu'(p. 73) on whom Monsieur Carré-Lamadon pins his hopes for the salvation of France, will not arise to redeem this corrupt society.

The sense of agitation and insecurity which characterises the story is sustained to the very end. By his presentation of the characters' outer selves in varied focus and clarity, the author creates a realistic portrayal of an event and of those who participated in it. The selected details which the narrator transmits to the reader result in an effect of impressionism which is

67

convincing because it has the hallmark of eye-witness news. At the same time, Maupassant endows his story with credibility by associating it with a known historical period, experienced at first hand by the original readers, and seeks to guarantee the accuracy of his narrative by supporting it with details of time and place.

By his revelation of the inmost thoughts of the characters, he proposes to the reader the attitude that he should adopt to the narrative whilst apparently leaving him to judge for himself. The combination of subject and narrative style results in a strangely affecting composition which provokes the reader and at the same time defies him to change the state of affairs. The duality of physical closeness to the actors in the story coupled with the distance of moral antipathy towards them is still producing its tension as we witness the final fade-out.

Conclusion

In her introduction to the Classiques Garnier collection of Maupassant's stories,' *Boule de Suif' et autres contes normands* , Marie-Claire Bancquart makes the point that until 1884-85 stories with settings in Normandy predominate in Maupassant's writing, and after that date tend to be replaced by scenes from Parisian life. There is no doubt that he was deeply attached to his Norman homeland, returning faithfully to Etretat or Fécamp in the summer, and visiting, until Flaubert's death in 1880, the city of Rouen and the master's house at nearby Croisset.

In the 'Etude sur George Sand', which was first published in 1884 as the preface to a collection of Flaubert's letters to George Sand, Maupassant describes the unending pleasure the great novelist took in the view from the window of his study of the shipping which passed so close to his house, the spires of Rouen's medieval churches and the modern "spires" of its factory chimneys, the surrounding meadows full of grazing cattle, and the forest of Roumare with the river winding peacefully along. The feelings are attributed to Flaubert, but the vivid expression of this spectacle is Maupassant's. In his work, examples are found in the brief but vivid hunter's impression sketched in *Le Garde* (*Œuvres complètes* , Vol 12, p. 236) and the more aesthetic response that can be attributed to Georges Duroy, a morally coarse individual not incapable of occasional sensitivity :

> On dominait l'immense vallée, longue et large que le fleuve clair parcourait d'un bout à l'autre, avec de grandes ondulations. On le voyait venir de là-bas, taché par des îles nombreuses et décrivant une courbe avant de traverser Rouen. Puis la ville apparaissait sur la rive droite, un peu noyée dans la brume matinale, avec des éclats de soleil sur ses toits, et ses mille clochers légers, pointus ou trapus, frêles et travaillés comme des bijoux géants, ses tours carrées ou rondes coiffées de couronnes héraldiques, ses beffrois, ses clochetons, tout le peuple gothique des sommets d'églises que dominait la flèche aiguë de la cathédrale, surprenante aiguille de bronze, laide, étrange et démésurée, la plus haute qui soit au monde.

(*Bel-Ami* , *Œuvres complètes* , Vol. 13, p. 321)

It is not unreasonable to suppose that his attachment to that landscape was as great as his appreciation of the beauty of the coast round Etretat and the harsher hinterland of the Pays de Caux, where he had spent his childhood. Madame Bancquart goes on to argue that his constant love for Normandy may be recognised by the fact that he returned to it in his writing when he was most under the stress of the tragic illness which finally overtook him. She notes that Maupassant's love of Normandy reappears in the story *Qui Sait ?* (1890) and the unfinished *L'Angélus* , begun in the same year.

Moreover, in *L'Angélus* as in *Boule de Suif* , the author returns not only to a place but to a specific date. Set outside Rouen, in the château of the Brémontal family, the story opens with an evocation of the extreme harshness of the winter of 1870. The young countess awaits her dinner guests and tries to repress her growing fears for her husband in the army, her family and her unborn child:

> Jamais elle n'avait senti peser sur elle encore une détresse aussi épouvantable. Qu'allait-il arriver de nouveau? Oh! l'affreux hiver, hiver de fin du monde qui détruisait un pays entier, tuant les grands fils des pauvres mères, espoir de leurs cœurs et leur dernier soutien, et les pères des enfants sans ressources, et les maris des jeunes femmes. Elle les voyait agonisants et mutilés par le fusil, le sabre, le canon, le pied ferré des chevaux qui avaient passé dessus, et ensevelis en des nuits pareilles, sous ce suaire de neige taché de sang.

> (*Œuvres complètes* , Vol. 29, p. 176 / 198)

The guests who arrive to dine with her have crossed the frozen river from the city and bring unwelcome news. Her father tells her that the Prussians have entered Rouen that very day, and that General Briand's men have fallen back. Another guest is able to provide more detail of what has happened in the city. He has seen the invading battalions gathering in front of the town hall and the day before he had watched as the French army retreated through Bourg-Achard.

In the course of the story, the countess's fears are realised. The enemy's brutal treatment causes her son to be born deformed, unable to walk. The suffering of this innocent victim and his mother's pain as she sees his rejection in the world become the theme of the incomplete middle section, and

70

the last fragments of the story convey an apocalyptic vision of suffering without redemption.

It is as if the author were once more recreating the catastrophe that he put at the centre of his story of *Boule de Suif* . In his final work, never completed, he returns to the preoccupation that had inspired his first success as a writer. It was not within even Maupassant's considerable gift as an artist to exorcise the intolerable memory of the day when news came that the Prussians would capture Rouen, and that General Briand's men had had to run for their lives.

Select Bibliography

BOULE DE SUIF

Neveux, P. (ed.) *Œuvres complètes de Guy de Maupassant* . Paris, Louis Conard, 1908-10, 29 vols. Volume 1, containing *Boule de Suif* , has a study of Maupassant by Pol Neveux, and much useful material, including correspondence, the article 'Comment ce livre a été fait', variants and extracts from reviews of *Les Soirées de Médan* , plus the short stories which preceded *Boule de Suif* . Volume 29, the second of those devoted to the *Œuvres posthumes* , contains the text of *L'Angélus* and notes. Considerable variations in pagination exist for this latter volume (see reference given in the Conclusion).

Bancquart, M.-C. (ed.) *'Boule de Suif' et autres contes normands* . Paris, Classiques Garnier, 1971. Informative introduction and notes. The letter in the appendix is particularly interesting. Useful bibliography.

Landers, W.M. (ed.) *'Boule de Suif' et autres contes de la guerre* . London, Harrap, 1982. Informative historical background and bibliography.

Dumesnil, R. (ed.) *Etudes, chroniques et correspondance.* Paris, Librairie de France [Gründ], 1938. Includes the 'Etude sur Emile Zola' of 1883 (pp. 76-88) and the 'Etude sur Gustave Flaubert' of 1876 (pp. 3-7), with a summary of all the short stories, plus a most handy 'Guerre de 1870' classification (p. 502).

Bolster, R. *'Boule de Suif* : une source documentaire?', *Revue d'Histoire Littéraire de la France* , LXXXIV (1984), 901-908.

LES SOIREES DE MEDAN

First edition by Fasquelle, Paris, 1880. Republished in Le Livre de Poche (1975), with the 1930 Preface of Léon Hennique.

Deffoux, L. et
Zavie, E.

Le Groupe de Médan . Paris, Crès, n.d..

CRITICAL WORKS

Dumesnil, R.

Le Réalisme et le Naturalisme . Paris, del Duca de Gigord, 1955.

Gershman, H.S. and
Whitworth, K.B.

Anthologie des préfaces des romans français du XIXe siècle . Paris, Union Générale des Editions, coll. '10/18', 1971—orig. ed., Julliard, 1965. Includes Maupassant's 'Etude sur le roman', Zola's 'Le Roman expérimental' and J.-K. Huysmans's preface to *A Rebours* . Extensive bibliography.

Steegmuller, F.

Maupassant : A Lion in the Path . London, Macmillan, 1972—orig. eds., New York: Random House, 1949, London: Collins, 1950.

Sullivan, E.D.

Maupassant : The Short Stories . London, Arnold, 'Studies in French Literature', nº 7, 1962, pp. 36-40.

HISTORICAL BACKGROUND

Bariéty, J. and
Poidevin, R.

Les Relations franco-allemandes 1815-1975 . Paris, Armand Colin, 1977. Chapters 3-5 are particularly relevant. A more specialized bibliography for historians concludes each chapter.